Cambridge Elements ☰

Elements in Language, Gender and Sexuality
edited by
Helen Sauntson
York St John University
Holly R. Cashman
University of New Hampshire

FEMINISM, CORPUS-ASSISTED RESEARCH, AND LANGUAGE INCLUSIVITY

Federica Formato
University of Brighton

CAMBRIDGE
UNIVERSITY PRESS

Shaftesbury Road, Cambridge CB2 8EA, United Kingdom

One Liberty Plaza, 20th Floor, New York, NY 10006, USA

477 Williamstown Road, Port Melbourne, VIC 3207, Australia

314–321, 3rd Floor, Plot 3, Splendor Forum, Jasola District Centre, New Delhi – 110025, India

103 Penang Road, #05–06/07, Visioncrest Commercial, Singapore 238467

Cambridge University Press is part of Cambridge University Press & Assessment, a department of the University of Cambridge.

We share the University's mission to contribute to society through the pursuit of education, learning and research at the highest international levels of excellence.

www.cambridge.org
Information on this title: www.cambridge.org/9781009517140

DOI: 10.1017/9781009236379

First published 2024

A catalogue record for this publication is available from the British Library.

ISBN 978-1-009-51714-0 Hardback
ISBN 978-1-009-23636-2 Paperback
ISSN 2634-8772 (online)
ISSN 2634-8764 (print)

Feminism, Corpus-Assisted Research, and Language Inclusivity

Elements in Language, Gender and Sexuality

DOI: 10.1017/9781009236379
First published online: October 2024

Federica Formato
University of Brighton

Author for correspondence: Federica Formato, f.formato@brighton.ac.uk

Abstract: This Element presents an investigation into the use of the gender inclusive schwa in a corpus of tweets; the schwa, is employed in Italian to overcome binary grammatical (feminine and masculine) morphological inflections. The investigation is set in a country where LGBTQIA communities still face institutional discrimination, yet it is contextualised in the growing work on inclusivity discussed in languages and contexts worldwide. The corpus is examined quantitatively and qualitatively, as well as read through a triangulation of two frameworks: Corpus-Assisted Discourse Studies and Feminist Critical Discourse Analysis. The findings, obtained from corpus-assisted research and digital ethnography, show that the new linguistic strategy is used creatively, functionally, and not exclusively as a self-representation tool, but is also a viable and powerful replacement for generic sexist language.

This Element also has a video abstract: www.Cambridge.org/ELGS_Formato

Keywords: gender inclusive language, gendered language, digital ethnography, CADS, FCDA

ISBNs: 9781009517140 (HB), 9781009236362 (PB), 9781009236379 (OC)
ISSNs: 2634-8772 (online), 2634-8764 (print)

Contents

1 Introduction to the Element   1

2 Gender-Inclusive Language in Italian   18

3 Triangulation and Reflexivity   61

   References   68

1 Introduction to the Element

This Element aims to explore the workings of gender-inclusive language, examining a corpus of tweets in Italian using linguistic strategies that overcome the binary grammatical and social system. The novelty lies in providing a systematic investigation into Italian and, more specifically, the schwa as a gender inclusive strategy; this is seen within the ever-growing literature on inclusivity and underlying reasons why language has a paramount role in societal changes with regard to gender and sexuality. Furthermore, I offer methodological and theoretical reflections by reading the results of the corpus investigation through a triangulation between Feminist Critical Discourse Analysis (FCDA) (Lazar, 2007) and Corpus-Assisted Discourse Studies (CADS) (Partington, Duguit, and Taylor, 2013).

1.1 Language, Gender, and Inclusivity

In my previous work *Gender, Discourse and Ideology in Italian* (Formato, 2019: 73), I argue that 'Italian counts 5 vowels (*a, e, i, o* and *u*) and *–u* would be the only one that could be introduced as neutral', while also discussing other strategies (e.g., *). At the time, I was not aware that (a) the *–u* was/is used in the attempt to resolve the binarism of the Italian language and (b) neutrality does not always equal inclusivity. In this Element, I aim to expand on (my) previous work as well as contribute to the emerging field of language inclusivity (in Italian and other languages). The long feminist tradition, started in the 1970s, that challenged the generic masculine(s) is not covered here due to space constraints. However, it is recognised as fundamental in the theoretical, methodological, and investigative apparatuses of this study (in Formato, 2019, I review key notions such as androcentrism, sexism, markedness, and feminism through seminal work, e.g., Cameron, 1995 and Mills, 2008).

In focusing on inclusive strategies beyond the binary, I believe it is important to briefly discuss the term 'inclusivity', conceived to cover many aspects – for example, teaching and learning, race, language diversity (including dialects), disability, and language testing. Here, I consider it in relation to gender and sexuality as conveyed through linguistic strategies. In this Element, I see inclusivity through the lens of morphological gender, which is typical of grammatical gender languages, including Romance ones (e.g., Italian, French, and Spanish). In addition, most languages will have options for considering and achieving inclusivity in relation to gender and sexuality through novel lexical items or syntactic strategies. To this, scholars have been paying attention, and the Gender in Language Project (collecting several languages, among others,

Catalan, Irish, and Tagalog) is only one example.[1] Morphological gender, in brief, refers to morphemes (meaningful units attached to a root) and how they are used to indicate gender (in Italian, morphemes also indicate singular and plural). Morphemes move from the unique grammatical function and become vectors of social gender (ideas, beliefs, attitudes), as explained in the comprehensive literature on language and gender. Traditionally, the morphemes were feminine, masculine, or comprehensive of both grammatical gender (epicenes); in some contexts (e.g., imbalanced workplaces), these morphemes were used in sexist ways – for example, generic masculines (see Formato, 2016, 2019 for Italian). On this topic, Sczesny, Moser, and Wood (2015: 944) argue that exclusive language, precisely generic masculines, 'has far-reaching consequences in restricting the degree of female visibility'.

Visibility has been a core aspect with respect to language and its expressions of social gender. In the search for visibility for women, those who worked on gender and language had as their primary goal to find solutions to *escape* the generic masculines, considering neutrality as one of the good options through words/expressions that would represent groups (e.g., *il corpo docente*/teaching body replacing *professori*/teachers or *professori e professoresse*/male and female teachers) or syntactic changes (e.g., *chi lavora con l'insegnamento*/ those who work in teaching). However, as research in this field evolved, as well as the awareness of speakers' selves, neutrality seems to dismiss (i) identity work in self-representation and representation of others; (ii) the expression of beliefs, ideas, and attitudes towards personal and social understandings of binary and non-binary gender. Therefore, neutrality and inclusivity are related, but they cannot be interchangeable in my view, specifically in the notion of motivation (Abbou, 2011), which are the *whys* we engage in some linguistic choices rather than others (I discussed this through concepts such as 'availability' and 'use' in Formato, 2019). Abbou (2011: 60) contemplates two options – that is, a language used to 'refer to human beings without distinguishing between what is clearly linked to the social gender of particular people and what is not' and 'using both the feminine or masculine forms when the reality being referred to includes both men and women', yet the terms 'inclusive/ inclusivity' are never mentioned. Returning to the notion of motivation, we must acknowledge that it would be challenging to measure the motivations of the speakers because these can be different from context to context and from interaction to interaction. However, we can reflect on why speakers (might) choose neutrality (e.g., *chi lavora*, those who work) or/over inclusivity (through morphological strategies) and vice versa. Clarity on terminology is thus needed,

---

[1] www.genderinlanguage.com/about.

whether about work done in the past to make women visible or the new efforts in a broader understanding of social gender and language. Concerning the former, the term 'gendered language' (as also discussed in Formato and Somma, 2023) has been used to describe the working of symmetrical uses of feminine and masculine forms, stemming from the *traditional* views of sexist language. Normativity, with respect to the binary (linguistically and socially), is central to this debate. Kolek (2022: 267) argues that the gender binary still occupies a major role and is regularly and steadily 'constructed, reproduced, naturalised and institutionalised'. Similarly, Leap (2003: 403) argues that 'gender is closely tied to assumptions of normativity that assign value to all forms of subject position within the social setting', urging ways to dismantle this normativity. Allen and Mendez (2018: 70) explain that 'heteronormativity has fundamentally, primarily, and historically privileged cisgender men and women, heterosexuality, and nuclear families', arguably portraying values meaningful across several cultures.

Efforts to disassemble and undo normativities, globally and glocally, are at the centre of inclusive language. To understand how inclusivity in language is being dealt with, I here provide an overview of the terminology discussed in the current literature; I then explain why 'gender inclusive language' is the term I chose for the study presented in Section 2. This term is not novel, as many other scholars have framed their work as gender inclusive language (in French, see Kosnick, 2019; in Spanish, see Bonnin and Coronel, 2021; Slemp, 2021; Slemp, Black, and Cortiana, 2020; in Slovene, see Popič and Gorjanc, 2018).

Gender inclusive language has also been used for languages categorised as *having* natural gender, such as English.[2] For instance, in the work by Pauwels and Winter (2006), the focus is on generic pronouns; similarly, the study of pronouns is also referred to as non-binary pronouns (Hekanaho, 2022; Konnelly, Bjorkman, and Airton, 2022) or epicene pronouns. Before the topic of inclusive language captured the full attention of some scholars, it was not unusual to see the labels 'anti-sexist' language (Lomotey, 2018), 'non-sexist' language (as suggested by Kolek, 2022), 'gender fluid' language (Lange, 2022), and 'gender-fair/er' language (Formato, 2019; Renström et al., 2022; in German *geschelechtegerecht*, Lange, 2022; in Swedish *könsmässigt spark* as reported by Bonnin and Coronel, 2021).

Écriture inclusif (EI, inclusive writing, Kosnick, 2019; Burnett and Pozniak, 2021) is used for French, where the focus is on the register in which it appears. The reference to writing seems paramount as one of the criticisms some

---

[2] The term 'natural' as in natural gender languages has been contested in more recent literature (Kinsley and Russell, 2024: 49) because it suggests that gender and sex are 'aprioristically construed as natural'.

inclusive linguistic devices receive is their unsuitability to be pronounced in spoken discourse (Formato and Somma, 2023). Phenomena in French and Spanish are also labelled *non-binaire* (Kosnick, 2019) and *non-binario*, respectively. Kolek (2022) also employs the term 'nonbinary Czech' (or, in the original language, *nebinární čeština*). These terms, in turn, focus on a more direct suggestion as to what linguistic devices can achieve: breaking the normative binary and moving to a (grammatical) non-binary system. It might also suggest that the devices are useful for some people, those who identify as non-binary, possibly foregrounding their self-representation. In further exploring the literature, I also came across the term 'pangender' (Sheydaei, 2021), yet exclusively referring to the third person singular pronouns, and Zimman (2017) uses the label 'trans affirmative language', focusing on how language can be part of an individual's transition. Kolek (2022) traces the steps of some other terms, such as 'nonheteronormative language', also used by Motschenbacher (2014) and 'gender-neutral language' (as in the case of Slovak). The former, 'nonheteronormative language', functions similarly to non-binary, as heteronormative is the gate that kept gendered identities (other than the cis women and men) outside, while the term 'neutral', in my opinion, seems to somewhat disregard social gender, as the term 'neutral/neutrality' might not reflect the nuances of a gender-loaded debate. Cordoba (2022) uses 'gender-neutral language' to justify his research on non-binary identities through interviews and corpus linguistics analyses. In other words, neutrality seems to refer to the linguistic work that some strategies do in removing and substituting the traditional grammatical morphological units (masculine and feminine). This interrogates us on the grammatical binary (masculine/feminine), constructed as the exclusive *carrier* of gender, therefore, suggesting that strategies such as the schwa in Italian (*–x/–e* in Spanish and Portuguese, or *point médian* in French) are neutralising gender in its entirety rather than portraying a different understanding of it (grammatically and socially). While theoretically valid, and an established term in the literature, the criticisms towards neutrality expressed here are exclusively aimed at rethinking how we can identify the connections of the language phenomenon mirroring the social contexts within the understanding of grammatical and social gender. I cannot exclude that 'gender-neutral' and 'gender-inclusive' might be perceived differently by the audience, yet I believe the word 'neutral' might miss some core points. Through this argument, I see 'non-gendered language' (Bonnin and Coronel 2021) as a similarly problematic term. Bogetić (2022a, 2022b) uses 'gender-sensitive language' in her work on Serbian, which I recognise as a valuable and viable alternative to 'gender-inclusive language'. It seems it could work even when translated into Italian, *linguaggio sensibile al genere*.

For reasons stemming from these reflections, I decided to use 'gender inclusive' language in this Element, as inclusivity is, in my opinion, an aspect of the deliberate efforts of the speaker in including people for long and, in many capacities, excluded.

I am aware that, in the Italian debate, the term 'inclusivity' has been approached with caution. Acanfora (2022), an author who writes on disability, autism, and neurodivergence, explains that

> il concetto di inclusione è discriminatorio in quanto suppone che il gruppo che include sia più potente o migliore di quello che viene incluso. È un atto che viene concesso e quindi può anche essere interrotto o revocato, sottolineando che il potere di accogliere le minoranze (e le condizioni a cui vengono eventualmente accolte) è nelle mani di chi include' (the notion of inclusion is discriminatory in that it suggests that the groups that includes is the more powerful or the best of those who are included. It is something that this group gives (to the less powerful group) that can be interrupted or revoked, highlighting that the power to welcome minorities (and the conditions to which these people are welcome) is in the hands of those who include). (my translation)[3]

While this is an important point, I think we can look at this narrative from a different point of view. Those who use language to include are more likely aware of the(ir) privileges, moving away from them, also by factoring in those who have been discriminated against in society; I wish to suggest that speakers choosing gender inclusive language have solid intentions. Furthermore, everyone can use and claim to use *linguaggio inclusivo*: people who are allying with the *cause*, people who do not recognise themselves in the binary, and those who, for many reasons, do not wish to associate themselves with binarism in grammatical gender. In some circumstances, those who work with the Spanish language have also proposed the term *incluyente* (one that includes) rather than *inclusivo* (inclusive), yet sometimes used only to refer to the inclusion of feminine nouns (or more generally, a language fairer to women).[4] In Italian, I have recently observed the use of *linguaggio ampio* (broad language) by Italian linguists and activists.[5] However, I argue that this does not embody the political relevance of what it means for the speakers and those who/what the speakers are foregrounding – that is, a world that is moving away from the binary as well as from its legacy (heterosexism and heteronormativity). While I believe that this discussion deserves more space, I here suggest that the

---

[3] www.fabrizioacanfora.eu/la-convivenza-delle-differenze.

[4] C. Guichard Bello (2015). *Manual de comunicación no sexista: Hacia un lenguaje incluyente.* Mexico City: Instituto Nacional de las Mujeres. http://cedoc.inmujeres.gob.mx/documentos_download/101265.pdf.

[5] https://rewriters.it/linguaggio-ampio-sette-spunti-piu-uno-per-allargare-il-campo.

differences and similarities of terms cannot be detached from the differences in how each language is grammatically organised, what context is under investigation, and what speakers are being examined. Similarly, Kinsley and Russell (2024) explain that terms may vary based on the project being carried out or on the researchers' positionalities and stances.

I also reflected on whether the hyphen or the lack of it could be considered meaningful; in other words, whether a choice between 'gender-inclusive' language or 'gender inclusive' had to be made, with the hyphen seen as creating a relationship between the two terms. Starting from what was discussed for Italian, 'gender-inclusive' language could signal that inclusivity is connected to gender in a more fine-grained way than, perhaps, non-hyphened 'gender inclusive' language. To conclude, I decided to use 'gender inclusive' language and 'gender-inclusive' language interchangeably and as comprehensive options for this study, where the schwa is mainly used as a generic strategy rather than one exclusively employed for self-representation (for which, possibly, 'non-binary language' would be more suitable). In addition to this, it also encapsulates the speaker's motivation (inclusivity). In the following subsection, I trace some core elements of the relation among inclusivity, language, and society.

1.2 The Relevance of Gender Inclusive Language

In this subsection, I aim to explore the theoretical underpinnings of gender-inclusive language, as these will be paramount to unravelling the investigation of its use in Section 2. I draw on the topic from a worldwide perspective, emphasising the common traits scholars have considered central in their work. This topic is gaining increasing attention: the Lavender Languages and Linguistics Conference 28, held at the University of Catania (Italy) in 2022, offered two parallel sessions and some other talks; at Lavender 29 in 2023, hosted at the University of Idaho (US), at least eight talks were discussing inclusive language (under different terminology) in several contexts (German, Danish, Spanish). In addition to this, the *Journal of Language and Sexuality* (volume 11, issue 2, 2022) published eight articles on non-binary language or (epicene) pronouns, and more recently, six chapters on pronouns and gender have been included in a handbook focusing on pronouns (Paterson, 2023). Moreover, the *Journal of Gender and Language* published an issue on gender inclusivity in language in Central and Eastern Europe (volume 16, issue 3, 2022).

In approaching the literature, one aspect comes to the fore: the many languages and contexts dealt with. More work is happening outside the anglophone academia, with many countries debating this topic in national circles and languages other than English (as is the case for Italian; see Section 2.3).

In a similar fashion, as it was/is for gendered language, visibility is central to the debate on gender inclusive language. With respect to this, there are two positions on visibility, one opposing the other: an extended visibility that opens to LGBTQIA+ communities and, for some, a visibility that excludes women. Most researchers, including myself, believe that extended visibility is an important step in granting legitimisation to people who are discriminated against on the basis of gender, sexuality, and gender identity.

Pershai (2017: 56) adds that, in making everyone visible, gender inclusive language is respectful and adequate; specifically, this new language 'gives a space' to people to recognise themselves. Similarly, Kolek (2022) suggests that inclusive language (referred to as nonbinary Czech) *creates* (the) space, adding an interesting layer to the debate, as *giving* could be seen as a concession of the most powerful groups (as debated earlier in this Element). The work by Pershai (2017) is mostly centred around language for transgender people and raises an important question: *Is inclusive language a solution?* I question whether having a yes/no answer would be useful, disregarding the complexity of societal forces, cultural nuances, and how language interacts and/or disrupts these.

In recognising that language can be *twisted*, even when meant to be inclusive, I convincingly argue that having options to make people visible is a step towards welcoming spaces for groups who have suffered, and still do, fierce discrimination at personal, family-related, and institutional levels. Similarly, Kolek (2022) sees the relation between language and society as paramount, arguing that a language that moves away from the binary does challenge traditional social perceptions of groups of people. Kinsley and Russell (2024: 35) define the links between the use of language and society as 'linguacultural' to mean context, but also specific ones (Italy, in my case).

It is worth mentioning that social forces, perceptions, and contexts cannot be exempted from politics and its ideologies. Bogetić (2022b: 5) explains how the debate around gender (and language) must be seen through the ideological currency (as in political terms) and the symbolic role, acknowledging that a sharp polarisation exists between those who embrace the notion of gender and those who fight against it. It is not surprising that more conservative political parties and those that are explicitly and implicitly far-right construct gender as 'a threat to the national fabric' (Bogetić, 2022b: 5). This is also defined by Borba, Hall, and Miramoto (2020) as the 'politics of enmity', borrowing the term and the underpinnings from Mbembe. Far-right groups and political parties *offer* to be 'self-identified guardians of good morals' (Borba et al., 2020: 3) in the fight against the enemy, the so-called gender ideology/gender theory. Similarly, Borba (2019), in investigating the use of the inclusive *-x* (*alunx*) in a Brazilian school, convincingly explains how (far-right aligned) opponents manipulate the use of this linguistic device to amplify discourses around threats to the status quo and *a* fear of difference. In unleashing such discourses, inclusive language is used, transnationally, by far-right populist groups to construct 'a moral panic' (Borba, 2019: 435) – that is, 'when some social phenomenon or problem is suddenly foregrounded in public discourse and discussed in an obsessive, moralistic and alarmist manner, as if it betokened some imminent catastrophe' (Cameron, 1995: 83).

Recently, the Conservative Party in the UK published an appeal to ban gender-neutral language as part of its campaign to attack transgender people and, in February 2024, the president of Argentina, Milei, banned gender inclusive language from official governmental documents.[6] Some Italian far-right activists are suggesting that Italy should consider similar actions, contributing to fuel anti-trans rhetoric (e.g., bathroom discourse). From a different political perspective, the liberal president of France, Macron, has explained the unnecessity of gender inclusive language. Concerning this transnational dimension, I find the term 'repatriarchalisation' (Bogetić, 2022a, 2022b) very useful; it suggests that newer ways to attack those who do not form part of the dominant group, or dominant policies, are developed to re-establish an order that still perceives masculinity as the main value. In Borba (2022), it can be seen how the narratives against a revaluation of gendered fixed roles flourish; it is indeed interesting that the terminology used to attack the revaluation is drawing on terms of their opposed communities as in the case of 'gender ideology' (called grafting; Bogetić, 2022b; Borba, 2022). Borba (2022: 60) explains this eloquently: '"Anti-genderists" creative semantic engineering appends their meanings onto well-established rights and anti-discrimination repertoires.'

Borba offers a comprehensive account of terminology and considers the terms anti-genderists use as a register, described as a 'conventionalised aggregate of co-occurring expressive forms and enactable person-types' (60). Institutions (such as the church), political parties, and mainstream media use this register.[7] The threat to the heteropatriarchal family is at the core of the attacks, specifically in countries such as Italy (as explained in Section 2). Biology-based claims are made to reaffirm the traditionally gendered status quo through 'the defense of an essentialist view of identity, sexuality and desire' (Borba, 2022: 67).

---

[6] www.boletinoficial.gob.ar/detalleAviso/primera/304017/20240226?busqueda=2.

[7] In March 2024, Pope Francis suggested that the most awful danger nowadays is gender ideology. www.lastampa.it/vatican-insider/it/2024/03/01/video/papa_francesco_lideologia_gender_e_il_pericolo_piu_brutto_del_nostro_tempo-14112293.

Transnationally, this defence is part of far-right parties' ideas about maintaining (and in some cases, rebuilding) a nation that is based on maternity, reproduction, and fertility, exclusively from the normative union between a woman and a man. In this, allyship emerges from the institutional and politically discriminatory messages and their worldwide proliferation, which still see the LGBTQIA+ community mistreated, violently attacked, and subject to many forms of bullying and brutality. In this climate, gender inclusive language functions as speakers' motivation to align themselves with the cause and is a deliberate message about where one stands.

In Borba (2019), the use of –*x* (in the educational setting investigated) can be seen through the notions of solidarity and humanity, where gender inclusive language can be seen as a common good (as in the words of the principal of the school). Similarly, Kolek (2022), in investigating speakers' use of non-binary Czech, refers to empathy towards people who feel discomfort with the traditional linguistic options for self-representation. Empathy is not only personal, and I conceive of this motivation as a collective action of those who 'espouse egalitarian ideals' (Ashburn-Nardo, 2018: 375); egalitarianism is here seen as the foundation of inclusion.

Radke et al. (2020: 292) provide an interesting taxonomy of four motivations for allyship, two of which are of interest to my analysis: specifically, *outgroup-focused motivations*, described as 'reflect[ing] a genuine interest in improving the status of the disadvantaged group', and *morality motivations*, 'where action is primarily driven by moral beliefs and a resulting moral imperative to respond'. *Personal motivation* can also arguably guide people in using gender-inclusive language. This is described as 'a desire to benefit oneself and meet personal needs by engaging in action for the disadvantaged group'. However, this is a much more cynical view of the notion of allyship and may be used to describe those actions, usually labelled *rainbow washing*, where companies are *exploiting* LGBTQIA+-friendly messages to gain public attention and, consequently, produce revenues.

The other type of motivation, *ingroup-focused motivation*, sees the support linked to maintaining the status of the advantaged group, which can be perceived as a similarly negative view of allyship. Positive and genuine allyship must be viewed in light of resistance work – that is, 'conscious, political and directed actions' (Radke et al., 2020: 293), as it will also be explained as a principle of FCDA (Section 1.3.2). In describing overt collective actions, Raby (2005: 153) argues that these are meant to oppose dominant power relations, 'with clear goals towards broad social change'.

However, an interesting point is made on the use of *Latinx*: Dame-Griff (2022) convincingly contends that while this term might be perceived as inclusive, it is intended to be exclusive. Specifically, *Latinx* is not intended to be used by everyone, especially with reference to the male–female binary. In the words of the author, it is an identity marker that 'can reflect years of grappling with issues such as discomfort with gendered norms and expectations, gender dysphoria, erasure within a binary system, and a personal and specific journey to understanding oneself beyond this binary system' (Dame-Griff, 2022: 125).

On the contrary, Scharrón-del Río and Aja (2020: 7) explain that this term 'includes all people from all genders, including those who do not fit the gender binary', de facto providing a definition that opposes the one of Dame-Griff with the mention of *all genders*, where those who do not fit the gender binary are an appendix to the main definition. This tension is a beneficial intellectual exercise as it pushes us to understand the impact of gender-inclusive language on some people and communities.

The version of Scharrón-del Río and Aja (2020) also posits that *Latinx* is an intersectional term, as it uncovers the discrimination people suffer from the perspective of gender and that of their migration status (whether first or further generation). Because of this, oppression is seen as systematic and structural, matching the original notion of intersectionality as put forward by Crenshaw (2017) and Hills-Collins (2019). Scharrón-del Río and Aja (2020) also trace an interesting connection between the –*x* as a gendered morpheme and its mean-ingfulness in Nahuatl culture, indigeneity, and blackness. *Latinx* is, therefore, 'a shift from casual and compulsory androcentrism', which is core in all uses of inclusive language (9). This, however, is a specific term and should be considered within the notion of liberatory praxis, which is meant to start a conversation around some people's past and present positions. Concerning allyship, *Latinx* 'has the potential for coalition building and organising on the grounds of solidarity toward social justice' (8).

What is clear is that *Latinx* and other gender inclusive uses are linked to an extension, or rather the defying, of known and traditional grammatical norms. Available scholarly work emphasises *social* significance over the fixed mor-phological, lexical, and syntactic rules. In examining options in Czech, Kolek (2022: 278) refers to this as the 'metalinguistic perspective of those who struggle with gendered structures in language and society'. As shown in Section 2, the formation of words that move beyond the binary grammatical structures also requires, according to Popič and Gorjanc (2018), knowledge about affixes and other ways of moulding linguistic devices. They believe language already had options to overcome the binary, namely how language could be made neutral (see Section 1.1 on differences among neutral, gendered, and inclusive language). Yet the point of foregrounding the social would be missed. The debate about innovation in language and other sociolinguistic underpinnings of language change is open. Banegas and Lopez (2021) explain that language change is normalised when speakers use the new forms 'naturally' and when these changes are not a factor of miscommunication.

In Section 2, the investigation will discuss these two accounts in a linguistic scenario that is new to the speakers/hearers yet quickly leaving its footprints in digital and more formal contexts. With regard to innovation, the case of pronouns is a telling one. While this debate does not necessarily concern the pro-drop Italian language, scholarly work on singular *they* in English as well as the gender-neutral *hen* in Swedish contributes to understanding the relations between these features and personal accounts and identities. In foregrounding the social aspect, Conrod (2020) recognises the relevance of respecting chosen pronouns as a matter of safety, considering discrimination and violence targeting those outside the traditional binary. Conrod (2022) provides a fascinating account of the multiple functions of singular *they*, as a generic and a specific pronoun, making gender relevant or irrelevant, as part of the expression of pragmatic principles (Grice's maxims) and politeness.

In the same special issue, Anderson (2022) and Melendez and Crowley (2022) create momentum about the social relevance of accepting, using, and teaching pronouns which are attentive to people's identities. Crowley (2022: 167) also raises an interesting point concerning the frequency, spread, and use of linguistic practices coming from linguistic activism: 'whether or not [they] are taken up by members of a community, these reforms are still seen as useful tactics for raising awareness and challenging hegemonic ideas about gender in language', fighting criticisms that still permeate the public debate around language, gender, and sexuality.

According to Hekanaho (2022), negative attitudes towards non-binary language are very similar to those that were found for gendered language, unravelling attitudes which go beyond grammar, the so-called *who is the master* (Cameron, 1995) and the accusation that only those who support gendered and non-binary language are ideological. In this respect, I have begun to reflect on the notion of nostalgia, considering the stark opposition from language academies (see Coady, 2022; Slemp, 2021) and from linguists. I link this to what was asserted previously: the gender war and repatriarchalisation. These are, in my view, connected to nostalgia.

Marchi (2022) discusses some key notions of nostalgia, borrowing the definition of a neuroscientist (De Brigand), containing cognitive, affective, and conative components. At the core of nostalgia is a *recuperation* of a mental simulation which could be either remembered or imagined (cognitive), the emotions coming from the memory and the distress for it to be the past (affective) and the restoration of positive properties of that past memory/mental simulation (conative).

In Borba (2019: 432), this is seen through the notion of mythopoesis, a 'supposedly remarkable past which is now under threat' – in brief, *the world we were*, or *the world we thought we were* (in the cognitive sense). However, this sentimentalisation of the past (Bonnett, 2016), whether accurate or part of individual or collective imaginations, seems to revolve around control (who is the master) and its re-establishment. The loss of this control in the narrative on *correct* language is central to the debate, especially for academies such as the French (Académie Française) and the Spanish (Real Academia Española) ones as well as the unofficial one in Italy (La Crusca). It is not new or exclusive to inclusive language, as gendered language suffered the same attacks (Formato, 2019) in the form of nostalgia for prescriptivist ideas of *the* social arrangement. The argument made here is amplified and perhaps gives us a chance to explore degrees of this nostalgia: it seems that some linguists and speakers have a nostalgia where the generic masculine was the only option. In contrast, others (such as the academies) suggest that the limits of gendered language are symmetrical feminine forms, de facto delegitimising gender-inclusive language. In addition, as Marchi notices, part of the debate on nostalgia is the possible distortion, manipulation, falsification, and unfactfulness of the imagined past to threaten the future. In Marchi's words, nostalgia is progressphobia.

In relation to progress, Calder (2022), in the plenary of the Lavender Languages and Linguistics Conference, raises a crucial point: a mismatch can occur between those who use the language to talk about the self through a certain perspective (the speakers), and those who are at the receiving end (the hearers) which might not have the tool or might not accept the speaker's (novel) perspective (especially when outside the cislingual point of view). While mismatches occur and are part of changing social and linguistic scenarios, I argue that the speaker needs to be put at the forefront of communicative events in self-representation and when gender is made relevant in its several capacities (including all, including some, excluding some). In Kinsley and Russell (2024), some aspects seem to emerge, offering an interesting and fruitful construction of *the* speaker/s. In admitting that personal and collective marry in communication, Kinsley and Russell (2024: 38) replace the term speaker/s with *languagers* (and *languaging* as a matching verb). These terms wish to suggest the dynamicity of language conveyed by the speakers as it 'continuously (re)create[s], (re)shape[s], and (re)articulate[s] their realities' (39), in an active effort to challenge a pre-established language (e.g., a fixed structure in grammatical gender languages). In the authors' view, this is linked to an equal dynamicity of gender, where the terms *genderers* and *gendering* aim to embody the active identity work (e.g., trans and cis modalities as in the argument by Kinsley and Russell, 2024). In previous paragraphs, we have seen how pre-established ways of conceiving gender and language have been and continue to be put forward, expressing nostalgia, creating a repatriarchalisation of values, used against LGBTQIA+ communities. I see this connected to what Kinsley and Russell conceive of as the perception that 'there is one correct way of enlanguaging realities' from a cislingual prescriptivism point of view (43).

This brief account of the theoretical underpinnings of gender-inclusive language has attempted to introduce valuable and fruitful tools to explain the analysis of a corpus of tweets presented in Section 2.

1.3 The Frameworks

In this section, I introduce the two frameworks I employ: Corpus-Assisted Discourse Studies (CADS) and Feminist Critical Discourse Analysis (FCDA), standing for *Corpus-assisted research* and *Feminism* in the title, respectively. The former offers a valuable tool to make patterns emerge from the corpus, and the latter provides a specific understanding of gender in language and in society. These frameworks have some commonalities and specific underpinnings and will be complemented by an in-depth reading of the findings emerging from the investigation that follows.

1.3.1 Corpus-Assisted Discourse Studies (CADS)

Corpus-assisted discourse studies is a methodological framework that moves the focus from the technicalities of the corpus investigation to the exploration of language in its relation to aspects of society and culture. Specifically, CADS 'seeks to capture the recurring traces left by social routines [where] the starting point is not linguistic but social' (Taylor and Marchi, 2018: 61).[8] That is, researchers could be motivated by issues of social justice (as reported by Baker 2018, in what he refers to as action research). While the combination of corpus linguistics and discourse is not new, the name CADS allows scholars to frame their work and be part of a research community. I do not mean to say that it is a rigid framework with a restricted community; on the contrary, it is a dynamic tool through which research can be conceptualised at the intersections between corpus linguistics and discourse. I am assuming that the readers

---

[8] Partington (2023) seems to distance himself from 'social' as one of the core elements of CADS, suggesting that this has covered several linguistic perspectives and theories (such as, to name a few, lexical priming and cohesion, pragmatics, literary stylistics), proposing that CADS concerns methodological choices.

are familiar with the debate on the notion of discourse; here, I borrow the explanation from the most recent publication on CADS (Gillings, Mautner, and Baker, 2023: 1): language is 'analysed as performing social functions'. Acarno (2020) also notes that CADS focuses on discourse studies rather than discourse analysis, with the scope of conveying the interdisciplinary nature of the framework. Here, I wish to bring some aspects to the fore: (i) the inclination to use CADS to explore social issues, (ii) its flexibility about where one positions their research on the two sides (Corpus Linguistics and Discourse Studies), and (iii) the implications of this concerning power and ideology/ies. I concur with what Taylor and Marchi suggest (2018: 61) in that CADS is interested in uncovering insights into a 'particular situation, purpose or function repeatedly enacted within a speech community'. The relation between society and language is seen in analytical explorations from text to discourse (Partington et al., 2013), in strict relation to what occurs in *the* society investigated through language phenomena, as well as in the simultaneous exploration at micro and macro levels (Acarno 2020). To do so, the quantitative aspect is not left without several in-depth qualitative remarks, which is why I choose this framework for analysing gender-inclusive language. The term 'quantitative' is perhaps a simplistic way to discuss some philosophical underpinnings such as recurring patterns, regularity, and, to some extent, what Partington et al. (2013: 10) refer to as serendipity. Recurring patterns tell us that what is happening might be *established* in the corpus as a representation of what is outside the corpus. Similarly, regularity can foreground what happens, putting the data set at the centre rather than the analyst who is called to interpret it rigorously. Differently, serendipity can 'show us things we perhaps didn't even know we didn't know' (Partington et al., 2013: 9), allowing the analyst to share insights with the scientific community and communities. For these reasons, building a CADS corpus means foregrounding the research's society-related scope while also maintaining the principles of representativeness – that is, selecting texts that are as relevant as possible to the phenomenon or the variety chosen. Partington et al. (2013) argue that one difference with corpus linguistics lies in CADS analysts exploring external data as a source of information to interpret but also to analyse the corpus. The corpus is not a black box (Partington et al., 2013: 12) but a source. The way in which this source is used to *extract* and interpret discourse is based on the flexibility of this framework, where research procedures, research goals, and, to some extent, levels of subjectivity are bespoke to each investigation. With regard to the opportunities and the affordances CADS offers, one can argue that it 'requires as much commitment to the computer-assisted profiling of corpora as to the human-led investigation of those discursive phenomena which are beyond the reach of automated analysis'

(Gillings et al., 2023: 7), where the analysts decide the ratio between the two based on the research question and the scope of the research (Acarno, 2020). I argue that the analysis of gender-inclusive language in this Element expands some of the assets of CADS – for instance, the reproduction of habitual patterns (Taylor and Marchi, 2018). My corpus is interested in how society deals with, embraces, and explores a new language phenomenon within a specific social (media) context. Furthermore, I conceive of the corpus as an ethnographic site (see Section 2), expanding on the notion of the relevance of the corpus in CADS investigations. In this brief overview, I attempted to present the main elements of this framework, and developments from these major points will be made across the Element. However, one aspect still deserves attention: in CADS tradition, discourse is not conceived of through a specific lens – for example, Historical Discourse Analysis or Critical Discourse Analysis. This should, therefore, not be seen as a shortcoming but rather an opportunity, as the one I wish to grasp here, to explore philosophical, methodological, and theoretical connections with established or new frameworks. For this reason, I considered studying the synergy with FCDA.

1.3.2 Feminist Critical Discourse Analysis (FCDA)

Feminist Critical Discourse Analysis has been theorised by Michelle Lazar (2005, 2007, 2014) and has gained some attention yet, I argue, it remains unexplored in language and gender (with some exceptions; see Nartey, 2024). I say gender because Lazar's work focuses on women and men as a starting point to explain how this framework can provide a platform for discussing contexts and language investigations. However, in her work, one can find room to expand, mould, or widen, if not the scope, the operationalisation of research. Lazar is firm in arguing that FCDA is not simply gender and Critical Discourse Analysis together, even though it borrows the focus on the complex workings of both power and ideology; FCDA foundations are patriarchal imbalances, gendered assumptions, and gender-related power asymmetries. In other words, these are not detached from the theoretical framework as they are embedded in it. In reworking feminist theoretical underpinnings, Lazar (2014: 182) explains, FCDA is deep-rooted in a 'feminist political imagination', allowing how society operates (mainly from a discriminatory point of view) to emerge in language investigations. Some principles are at the core of FCDA, which I see aligned with the research proposed here. The first principle, feminist analytical activism, is about conducting research not only to talk about the material consequences of the imbalances to take but to see the published work '*as* action' (185). The second principle, gender as ideological structure and practice, is based on the notion that society is divided into gendered groups, not based on biology but on values associated with men and women and, in my work, on a broader understanding of gender and sexuality that moves away from the binary. These two principles are fundamental to understanding how this Element relates to the reality outside academia and research, as well as my positioning as a feminist scholar. The third one, the complexity of gender and power relations, is central to what I am exploring in this Element. While in the first two, Lazar emphasises discourses of covert or overt discrimination (e.g., sexism) to explore in the language used in a specific cultural context, the third one opens to discourses of resistance and challenge to the status quo, which, in my view, is what gender-inclusive language sets out to do. Lazar recognised that this side of the framework had not paid equal attention to discourses of discrimination, making it an opportunity for the research conducted here to expand on the usefulness of FCDA. Resistance and challenge discourses must be seen as empowering and situated in a specific, large or small site of struggle. The fourth principle, discourse in the (de)construction of gender, builds a bridge between this framework with theoretical underpinnings such as poststructuralism (briefly put, language is a resource which is socially shaped); in addition to this, Lazar mentions the relevance and salience of allyship, yet not using this term. In the discussion of this principle, mentions of methods are given; as in the tradition of other critical studies, FCDA does not recommend a specific method or methodology, as it is concerned more closely with how the findings are read in the analysis of the social, cultural, and political context. The last principle, critical reflexivity as praxis, is linked to the first one in that it asks the researcher to transfer the knowledge in a variety of modus operandi and several contexts, providing a 'rich and powerful critique for action' (Lazar, 2007: 144). Considering these five principles, one can see how FCDA puts gender at the centre of research, allowing researchers to continue the tradition beyond known gender and sexuality binaries. In Section 1.3.3, I briefly discuss what triangulation is and how I move to achieve so based on the two frameworks, CADS and FCDA.

1.3.3 Triangulating CADS AND FCDA

This Element proposes a novel synergy between the two frameworks outlined previously, aiming to use their strengths to explain the findings. While the term 'synergy' gives the idea of connection, studies in linguistics (and other fields) use the term 'triangulation'. This is not new, as some underpinnings explained here will suggest, but notable differences can be found across disciplines. Egbert and Baker (2020) state that triangulation 'is a research approach that takes two or more perspectives'. Bazeley and Kemp (2012: 55) argue that the approaches must have 'a common purpose that goes beyond that which could be achieved with either method'. This is paramount in this research: by reading the findings through these two frameworks combined, I wish to offer a close account of what happens when gender inclusive language is used. Flick (2017) convincingly pinpoints one core value, borrowing from Denzin (1970-[1978]) – that is, triangulating is a strategy of validation, and its use carries a maximisation of validities in the fields of inquiry concerned. Validating is intended here as a seal of consistency in reviewing the findings according to theoretical and methodological tools. While many (in corpus linguistics studies, see Egbert and Baker 2020) have worked towards a taxonomy of triangulations – for example, methodological, theoretical, and investigator – I am here faced with a mixed triangulation; FCDA is mainly theoretical, while CADS focuses on fruitful corpus techniques in investigating social issues. It is, in my view, the reason why these two triangulate robustly: this research did not wish to be an investigation of language, gender, and sexuality through corpus tools (and its techniques) but instead to have gender (as a broad term) as a core justification for the choice of topic, data, methods, and analysis. In other words, FCDA complements the examination of social issues (as for CADS focus) by providing a rationale for the researcher and for what emerges in the imbalanced site of struggle in which language, but primarily, gender (as an umbrella term) operates. The traces to investigate through CADS in a particular situation are for FCDA the structures in which there are asymmetries, assumptions, and resistance related to gender. In other words, the linguistic performance of social action in CADS is found in these deep-rooted workings of gender in society. They cannot be seen as separate from a historical legacy.

Furthermore, in both frameworks, the researcher has an active role in engaging (through the analysis and for FCDA in praxis) with the social topic from a justice point of view. The micro and macro levels (as for CADS investigations) are related to the fourth FCDA principle, that of deconstruction. In addition to this, CADS allows the analyst to choose the inclination to more corpus-relevant findings or discourse findings. FCDA is employed here to resolve the balance between the two (as seen in the analysis of functions, Section 2.5.3). With FCDA being theory-focused (not recommending any methodological framework) and CADS being more method-focused (not recommending any theoretical framework), I believe that some interesting parameters attributed to methodological triangulations might be challenging to apply – for example, convergent or correlational, independent, sequential or cyclical (for an overview see Egbert and Baker 2020). The triangulation here is more closely related to contributions in social science studies in that the goal is to 'add breadth or depth to our analysis' (Fielding and Fielding, 1986: 33) and, as Flick (2017) suggests, to understand how the perspectives, placed side by side, are valuable and influential in the production of extra knowledge.[9] I will operationalise the underpinnings of FCDA and CADS in Section 3, providing corpus-assisted analysis of patterns, metalanguaging, and functions related to using the gender-inclusive strategy of the schwa in Section 2.

2 Gender-Inclusive Language in Italian

To investigate how gender inclusive language occurs in a specialised corpus of tweets, I begin by highlighting different layers with regard to context. I start by explaining Italy through the political efforts in favour of as well as obstacles faced by LGBTQIA+ communities. I then move to the linguistic context, which would be seen in a vacuum without exploring Italian society and culture. The last part of this section is dedicated to academic studies on the Italian language and some reflections by linguists shared with/on the media. In the second part of the section, I present the corpus, how it was built and investigated; then, I examine the corpus from several quantitative and qualitative angles.

2.1 The Social Context

Before I explain how inclusive devices work in Italian, I briefly contextualise Italy in relation to gender and sexuality from social and cultural perspectives, offering some justifications as to why I investigate this specific linguistic phenomenon in this context. Italy is a country that has been considered highly sexist (Callahan and Loscocco, 2023; Formato, 2019; Hipkins, 2011), where fixed gender roles for women and men are at the centre of the family as a political institution. Specifically, I concur with Callahan and Loscocco (2023), who flag the Italian traditional family model – that is, the heterosexual couple – as a powerful institution that reproduces *natural* distinctions for gender roles. Together with the concept of family, the church still has a 'powerful grip' (as suggested by Benozzo, 2013) on Italian citizens' political and cultural life. I do not intend to say that the country does not react to conservativism but that the forces which aim for a change do not find, in most cases, political or institutional legitimisation. For instance, the Partito Democratico (Democratic Party) (PD) lost the battle to have a proposal bill pass in the parliament during a government (in power from February 2021 to October 2022) led by Mario

---

[9] In social science research, there seems to be a fierce confrontation between quantitative and qualitative methods, with triangulation mainly proposing that mixed methods can offer a resolution, with a sub-field of inquiry labelled mixed methods research (MMR). I wish to refer to the discussion only tangentially and borrow knowledge that helps explain what is being attempted in this Element.

Draghi, the former president of the European Central Bank; Draghi was called to help Italy navigate the difficult months of the Covid-19 pandemic and an economic crisis, having no political mandate to *look after* other issues. His was a technocratic government, with a majority consisting of many (and opposing) parties, such as the PD (left wing), FI (Forza Italia, right wing), Movimento 5 Stelle (5-Star Movement, arguably, centre), Italia Viva (centre) and Lega (League, far-right). Fratelli d'Italia (Brothers of Italy, far-right) was the only party that sat at the opposition. The law called Legge Zan (from the name of the MP who initially proposed it) was aimed at extending another law, called Mancino (from the name of the MP who proposed it in 1993), punishing hate crimes based on race, ethnicity, religion, and nationality. The Legge Zan was titled Misure di prevenzione e contrasto della discriminazione e della violenza per motivi fondati sul sesso, sul genere, sull'orientamento sessuale, sull'identità di genere e sulla disabilità (Preventive and contrastive measure against violence and discrimination based on sex, gender, sexual orientation, gender identity and disability) and aimed at tackling homophobia and transphobia, but also disability (a topic many ignored during the media and parliamentary debates). The Camera dei Deputati approved the law on 4 November 2020; it was then brought to the Camera del Senato for discussion and to be voted on. Here, the proposed bill found many obstacles, as the Commissione Giustizia (a committee that itemises the bills to discuss), led by right-wing politicians, failed to diarise the discussion in the chamber. On 27 October 2021, with secret voting, the law did not pass because of a technicality (called *non passaggio all'esame degli articoli* based on article 96 of the Senato regulations, meaning that some senators could suggest that the law should not be discussed).[10] One hundred fifty-four senators voted in favour of the non-discussion versus one hundred thirty-one who voted against it. What followed consisted of accusations among parties, especially among the centre and the left, with the PD accusing Italia Viva of having voted not to discuss the bill. The accusations were based on Italia Viva's battle to have the notion of gender identity removed. In addition to this, the Vatican had allegedly sent a letter to protest, suggesting that the law would violate the *Concordato* (an agreement between the church and the Italian state) on the notion of 'libertà di pensiero' (freedom of thought); so-called pro-life and other Catholic groups had also voiced their unfavourable opinions. The failure to pass this law must be seen in relation to what I argue is the central point in Italian culture – that is, 'the symbolic and material power of Italian masculinity' (Callahan and Loscocco, 2023: 9). From this, women and other gender groups are seen as inferior and as opposed to the most powerful social and cultural

---

[10] www.senato.it/istituzione/il-regolamento-del-senato/capo-xii/articolo-96-1.

identity. Not only cis heterosexual men but also a politics that is sexist, homophobic, and transphobic, supported by the media, means that traditional beliefs are embodied and not successfully challenged. The current government is led by Giorgia Meloni (2022–present), the first female *Presidente del Consiglio* (prime minister), and it is a far-right one that sees Fratelli d'Italia governing together with Forza Italia and Lega.[11] In her past campaigns as well as current affairs, there has been a push to re-establish traditional views of gender, reworking towards a social order that considers men and values associated with them as central to society. These ideals are shared by the entire far-right coalition (Fratelli d'Italia, Lega led by Matteo Salvini and Forza Italia led by Antonio Tajani). On this topic, Evolvi (2023: 2806) explains the connections between anti-gender movements and Italian political parties through 'a transnational populist mobilization against the perceived threat of gender ideology' – for example, when Matteo Salvini (currently the minister of transport and infrastructure) and Prime Minister Giorgia Meloni gave a speech at the pro-family World Congress of Families in 2019. Their stance is *typical* of populist far-right politics, one concerned about the threat to the *natural* family and, consequently, to the nation.[12] Specifically, the political unit of the family is seen through a lens that favours homogeneity in terms of religion and ethnicity (Evolvi, 2023), therefore foregrounding xenophobia and Islamophobia together with homophobia and transphobia. In this context, gender-inclusive language emerges as a resistance imaginary of a different society yet receiving constant backlash from the far-right (and silence from the left) that reframes this in relation to moral panic and nostalgia (see Section 1.2).

2.2 The Linguistic Context

Italian is a grammatical gender language and has a gender system in place which allows for morphemes or suffixes to make gender visible. However, this visibility (as shown in Formato, 2019) is traditionally binary, masculine or feminine, and when seen through the social lens, it could be sexist or imbalanced. For these reasons, speakers of Italian found alternatives aimed at moving beyond

---

[11] Unsurprisingly, Giorgia Meloni announced that she wishes to be addressed with the masculine form, *il presidente*.

[12] In March 2023, an official document issued by Minister of Interior Matteo Piantedosi demanded institutions (such as city councils) to stop including non-biological parents on birth certificates of those born through surrogacy. In the document, one reads that surrogacy 'offende in modo intollerabile la dignità della donna e mina nel profondo le relazioni umane' (unendurably offends women's dignity and deeply undermines human relations). Those affected, having only the biological parent recognised, are left facing consequences that range from school to healthcare rights, this complementing the ongoing delegitimisation of same-sex couples and LGBT families (also referred to as famiglie arcobaleno/rainbow families). https://www.gay.it/famiglie-arcobaleno-meloni-piantedosi.

Table 1 Linguistic inclusive devices used in Italian

Strategy	Example
asterisk *	ragazz*
schwa ə (singular) and long schwa ɜ (plural)	ragazzə, ragazzɜ
–u	ragazzu
–@	ragazz@
X	ragazzx

this grammatical and social binary. The linguistic devices found to overcome binarism (shown in Table 1) are not standardised, which means that they are not included in grammar books, and more could appear in the future to substitute those employed nowadays. Primarily, they can be used for words that are part of the morphological gender (root + morpheme) classification and, to some extent, for those classified as syntactic gender (root + one morpheme for both feminine and masculine surrounded by gendered satellite elements), rather than those in the lexical gender classification (e.g., *madre*/mother and *padre*/father which neutral terms, e.g., *genitore*/parent can replace), with some exceptions.

The table simplifies the complexity of *creating* a language that overcomes the binary. Examples such as these present the common solutions allowed in the gender system: adding a morpheme (*, @, x, ə) to the root (*ragazz–*). This replaces (i) gendered vowels (commonly, *–a*.fem.sing, *–e*.fem.plur, *–o*.masc. sing, *–i*,masc.plur) or (ii) gendered compounds, as explained later. I here refer to gender-inclusive devices as morphemes as, in my view, these symbols are meaningful for those who use them, regardless of their *official* position in standard grammar. With the morphemes being 'the minimal linguistic units with a lexical or a grammatical meaning' (Booij, 2012: 8–9), one can see how the inclusive devices are used according to the traditional notion of attaching the vowel to the root. This entails that speakers might have morphology knowledge, complying with some known rules even for new, non-standard, and creative phenomena (Booij, 2012: 4). As for the strategies in Table 1, the schwa seems to be the most frequent, replacing the * which I seemed to have noticed was preferred in the previous years.[13] The different strategies not only exist on their own rights but they can also coexist. For instance, Burnett and Pozniak (2021), in

---

[13] However, in a conversation with Somma (private communication, 2023), there seems to be an imbalance between the schwa and *, where the latter might have a more deep-rooted symbolic value for specific communities (such as trans communities or in the case of *Non una di meno*), with the schwa arguably becoming a more popular symbol.

their study of university brochures, found that several forms of gender inclusive language were used (point médian, hyphen, period, etc.) in French.

In retracing the history of the schwa, Sulis and Gheno (2022) mention the efforts of Luca Boschetto, who, in 2015, launched the schwa through the website *italiano inclusivo*, as well as the ramifications of Boschetto's indications in printing (e.g., the publisher Effequ, specific comics, newspaper articles).[14] Gheno (2022: 192) points out that the schwa can be used for a group of people, a person of unknown gender, or a non-binary identified person. This means that the schwa (and possibly the other inclusive devices) functions as (i) a generic tool replacing versatile/generic masculines (Formato 2019) – that is, those terms in their masculine form used to refer to a group of people of mixed gender – and (ii) a specific tool used to talk about people's gender identity or one's own. These two functions are very different: in (i), the gender of the referents is *hidden* in a mixed gender group where the speaker's stance towards social beliefs around gender is embedded in the choice of inclusive language; in (ii), gender is made visible, whether it is used by someone who refers to another person or is used for self-representation. Russell (2024: 277) seems to cast a doubt that these two functions are connected in creating an inclusive space, questioning whether the generic function is exclusively seen as erasing the binary without 'realising any identity beyond it'. I argue that, in these cases, it is the speaker, through the language, that is creating this space/ imagination away from the traditional binary, even when not addressing a specific gender-related identity of an individual. Regarding grammar, there are a few issues with the formation of words with more complex suffixes (introduced in Formato and Somma, 2023). For instance, words which are formed with the compound *–trice* (fem.sing) and *–tore* (masc.sing) are problematic, as they could result in a non-intelligible form; it is the case of words such as *senatrice* (fem.sing/female senator)/*senatore* (masc.sing/male senator), which could become senatə. While I have not encountered any occurrence of this, I have noticed (see corpus description) inclusive devices attached to the masculine form – for instance, *autorə* (*autore*.masc/*autrice*.fem, autor), *scrittorə* (*scrittore*.masc/*scrittrice*.fem, writer) – these are also unproblematically used by Gheno (2022).[15]

Gheno (2022: 188) reports that words such as these – for instance, *sostenitorə* (supporter) – 'non presenta[no] nulla di incoerente' (do not present any incoherence), as some words seem to have two feminine endings in *–trice* and *–tora*. However, *scrittora* appears only once in the dictionary Treccani (one of the

[14] https://italianoinclusivo.it.
[15] www.treccani.it/magazine/lingua_italiana/speciali/Schwa/4_Gheno.html.

major vocabularies in Italy and one dedicated to gendered issues) and to describe a specific writer, while *autora* never appears.[16]

Another aspect is the use of the schwa with the plural of words that end in c+masculine morpheme or ch+feminine morpheme – for instance, *amici* (masc. plur, friends) and *amiche* (fem.plur, friends), seen as appearing in several forms *amicǝ, amichǝ*. Similarly, psychologist/therapist could be problematic as the plural form splits depending on the feminine (*psichologhe*) or the masculine (*psicologi*). This means there is some tension in the formation of words, specifically in the preference to use masculine roots to which the inclusive morpheme is attached, as well as phonological technicalities (see Safina, forthcoming). Interestingly, Popič and Gorjanc (2018) comment on the (generic) speakers' knowledge of affixes and suffixes in the formation of gender inclusive words, which does not necessarily follow strict and standard grammatical rules.

In her book, Gheno (2022: 195) lists some recommendations, in perhaps a prescriptivist way, among which are:

- The articles to use – that is, *lǝ* for singular nouns and *ǝ* for plural ones (also discussed in Sulis and Gheno, 2022);
- Use of *ǝ* for words such as *atleta* (athlete, referred to in my work as belonging to syntactic gender, Formato, 2019), except for where the schwa exclusively substitutes the plural morphemes (what I refer to as semi-epicene, 2019) – for example, *pediatre* (fem.plur), *pediatri* (masc.plur) becoming *ǝ pediatrǝ*;
- Use of the simplified *preposizioni articolate* (i.e., when articles and prepositions are combined) – for example, *allǝ/dellǝ bambinǝ* with singular nouns and *aǝ* and *deǝ* for plural nouns – for example, *aǝ/deǝ bambinǝ*.[17] From this example, one aspect that can be noted is that the long schwa, proposed by Luca Boschetto, is possibly not preferred over the short schwa, which signals both the singular and the plural.

The analysis that follows examines these forms, as these recommendations were not part of a systematic analysis.

The schwa and other gender inclusive strategies form part of speakers' motivation, acknowledging changes in society and how these are accommodated through language (specifically in written registers); this can be seen through what is believed relevant and/or fair and how, broadly, we aim to

---

[16] There are some words that end in *–tora* – for example, *esattrice/esattora* – or some that exclusively end in *–tora*, as for instance, *questora*, a term which is not very much in use, since the masculine (*questore*) is preferred as a generic. For these terms, it could be possible to replace the final vowel with the schwa – for example, *questorǝ*.

[17] I decided not to attribute an English translation to the *preposizioni articolate* as this linguistic item belongs to Italian grammar.

position ourselves concerning social issues. For instance, I find very powerful (despite some criticisms I observed on social media), the use of *sorellǝ* (*sorellǝ non sei solǝ*, sister you are not alone) by *Non Una di Meno*. They use a grammatically feminine term (belonging to the category of lexical gender), *sorella*, in its inclusive form to include, in my view, more than what we might consider traditional femininity/womanhood. Similarly, they use *transfemministǝ* (transfeminist) instead of the epicene *transfemminista*.

In a recently published interview (Sulis and Gheno, 2022: 168), Gheno suggests that 'for now, the schwa cannot be seen as the ideal solution to the problem of inclusivity in language', referring to it as an experiment that might lead to *better* solutions. The investigations in the following sections aim at understanding how speakers use and conceptualise this solution.

2.3 The Academic Debate

The use of masculine forms to address women, specifically in male-dominated environments such as politics, law, and healthcare, has been widely documented (see Formato, 2014, 2016, 2019, forthcoming; Formato and Tantucci, 2020; Nardone, 2018; Maestri and Somma, 2020). Gender inclusive language has only recently been paid attention to, and investigations of data are slowly emerging. There seems to be a divide between senior linguists, who were interested in the feminisation of titles, and others, among whom are junior ones (i.e., PhD students), who seem more open to examining the functioning of the schwa and other gender inclusive devices. This section attempts to explain the two views while also considering the importance of investigating new phenomena and their relationship with a changing society.

In commenting on this debate, Sulis and Gheno (2022) and Formato and Somma (2023) discuss some opposing views, such as that of the linguist Giusti, who suggests that the schwa could lead speakers to *interpret* it as a masculine morpheme for prestigious and non-prestigious terms. Similarly, the view of the linguist Robustelli, reported in the interview, suggests that inclusive language renders women invisible. In Thornton (2022: 49), one reads that using the schwa as an 'esplicito obiettivo politico' (explicit political goal) might not serve the interests of some groups – for example, those who promote feminine forms. These views suggest that the hearer's interpretation is more important than the speaker's motivation (see Section 1), primarily from an inductive perspective, as no naturally occurring patterns have been systematically investigated in their work. Furthermore, I frame this as an ideological position with regard to what inclusive language might serve and is linked to scholars' ideas and beliefs around social gender. One of the opposing linguists, Arcangeli, published a petition on Change.org to stop the schwa from being used in universities and official documents (in a similar vein of the political bans in school or institutions in Brazil, see Borba 2019). The petition addresses a non-specified audience which he wishes will take action.[18] The title, *pro lingua nostra* (in favour of our language), seems to translate those nostalgic feelings of nationhood and nationalism discussed in Section 1, proper to populist views. The text is also reminiscent of accentism/linguicism, which is discrimination based on varieties spoken (Paterson, 2019), where the schwa is seen through the lens of those dialects, all from the south, that include it in their repertoire (see also Formato and Somma, 2023 and Section 2.5.3); Russell (2024) also believes that discriminatory views are to be taken into consideration when the schwa is associated with southern areas.

Arcangeli is not new to exhibiting his doubts about the schwa. He published two books, mainly meant for non-academic audiences, where he proceeds to *mock* the schwa in the volume *La lingua Scəma: Contro lo Schwa (e Altri Animali)* (*The Stupid Language: Against the Schwa and Other Animals*) and political correctness, in *Una Pernacchia Vi Seppellirà: Contro il Politicamente Corretto* (*A Raspberry Will Bury You: Against Political Correctness*).[19] In an interview on *Il Giornale*, a right-wing newspaper, Arcangeli touches upon some criticisms also put forward by La Crusca, the unofficial language academy of the Italian language.[20] In brief, the criticisms are: (a) feminisation of titles is at risk (Arcangeli suggests that 100 feminine terms are threatened); (b) inclusive language is an ideological matter; (c) inclusive language cannot be systematically employed and gender agreement is lost in elements other than the inclusive noun; (d) the debate is (seen as) an imposition from a minority (seemingly the LGBTQIA+ community). While I will go back to some of these points in the examination of the corpus, I argue it is here important to touch on (a): by suggesting that inclusive forms such as *tutt**, *tuttu*, *tuttə* (everybody) hide all women could signal an ideological position that only considers women within the traditional binary, disregarding that people might choose to address themselves and wanting to be addressed with the feminine, the masculine, or, in several capabilities, with inclusive language, as is the case of (some) non-binary people. On this account, Cordoba (2022: 5, my emphasis) suggests that 'non-binary' 'is often used as an umbrella term for individuals who may identify as

---

[18] www.change.org/p/lo-schwa-%C9%99-no-grazie-pro-lingua-nostra.

[19] Here the term 'raspberry' is used with the informal meaning of 'a *rude sound* made by *stick ing* the *tongue* out and blowing' (my emphasis). https://dictionary.cambridge.org/dictionary/english/raspberry.

[20] www.ilgiornale.it/news/cronache/linguista-arcangeli-schwa-distrugge-litaliano-dallinterno-2010894.html.

and/or express: no gender, *two genders*, a partial gender, an additional gender, a fluid gender, and/or a political and/or personal gender that disrupts the gender binary'. Therefore, to claim that all women are rendered invisible with gender inclusive terms is to have a restricted view of gender, one that language inclusivity aims at defying. Furthermore, it focuses on prescriptivist views of what should be available to the speakers and what linguists think this means for those who use these forms.

Moving on to other work done on gender inclusive language, Rosola (in preparation) uses the term 'structural misgendering', explaining that the Italian language seems to *lack* resources to address inclusivity. However, work such as this demonstrates that language is never detached from its speakers and that avoiding references to gender or including people regardless of their gender was possible even before speakers experimented with new symbols/morphemes (e.g., through collective nouns). In her interesting work, she explains that when *tutt** is used 'gender is neutralised' (Rosola, in preparation). I see this in contrast with the triple splitting *tutt**, *tutte, e tutti*, where gender is made visible according to the author. I argue that both forms are inclusive and give some indications about speakers' alignment to gender, which is discussed as a concept. With the aim to categorise strategies, González Vásquez, Klieber, and Rosola (forthcoming) discuss three major groups of strategies in German, Spanish, and Italian: (i) visibility (including splitting, gendering, slash, and generic feminines); (ii) gender-neutrality (including neutral plural forms, fixed gender forms, semi-epicenes with no gendered elements, collective nouns, and avoidance strategies); and (iii) innovative strategies (including a list of morphemes or other devices as discussed earlier in this Element). Their lists are comprehensive and extensive; for instance, –*ai* is proposed as a linguistic device for inclusive plural forms in Italian (however, no example is provided). As regards the second category (gender neutrality), one should question whether neutrality is indeed meant to include or exclude gender, having to choose between the terms 'gender neutrality' and 'neutrality', as no gender elements are included. Similar to this, Thornton (2022), uses the terms *neutralizzare* (neutralise), *neutralizzazione* (neutralisation), and *strategie di neutralizzazione* (neutralisation strategies) in commenting on the schwa and its *place* within the grammatical system. Equally, Safina (forthcoming) frames her work as neutralisation. As widely described in Section 1, I continue to question the sociolinguistic value of this notion (and its derivates) in contrast to gender-inclusivity that, in my view, encapsulates what the schwa and other symbols are socially, politically, and ideologically *doing*. On this topic, Russell (2024) discusses the complexity of language choices and their relation to personal and collective views on gender in Italy, investigating language used to describe a transgender person killed by their brother. Among the many interesting points made, I wish to foreground the perceived negativity, what Russell explains as a 'negationist frame', in giving inclusive language a chance. Based on what was suggested previously, what is negated here is not only language but also *untraditional* understanding and realisation of gender as a part of people's identity. Specifically, 'when languagers are not given access to possible spaces in which to participate, freedom is shackled. When the enlanguagements of a minority are deemed inadmissible or dangerous, freedom – including that of the majority – is atrophied' (Russell, 2024: 295). In 'not given access', we have seen how linguists, based on personal beliefs, contribute to restricting freedom, language, and participation in social space, covering this with sociolinguistic mystification. This is not new, as I found similar opinions and views when I investigated gendered terms, referred to as *ad personam* sociolinguistic knowledge (Formato, 2019). This begs for investigation of language used by speakers in formal and informal contexts, re-establishing the power where it is held and can be exercised. This point is also made central in Conrod (2022), who suggests that some inaccurate scientific information related to personal biases is spread. Similarly, Konnelly et al. (2022: 134) suggest that these views could 'cloak erroneous transphobic arguments in a veneer of intellectual valid-ity'. I concur with Conrod (2022) in that collecting, exploring and investigating data is the way to resolve generalised personal grammatical intuitions, such as those used in the public debate, by linguists and others, on gender inclusive language. For instance, concerning the *, Pierucci (2021) conducted a qualitative yet very limited analysis showing how some inconsistencies still appear when the * is used but suggests that young people are more accepting of this inclusive device in platforms targeting them.[21] Safina (forthcoming) and Facchini (2021) are contributing to the investigation of gender inclusive lan-guage in several contexts, highlighting the complexity of these language phe-nomena but also their social, political, and professional potential. Safina investigates four transfeminist Facebook pages (connected to *Non Una di Meno* activism) and has found that the schwa is increasingly used in the chosen time frame. At the same time, other symbols, such as the asterisk and –*x*, tend to decrease. Gender inclusive strategies are used in several parts of speech (mostly pronouns such as *tutt* –). The discussion also includes examples of mismatches in gender marking. Gender-inclusive devices are useful and become meaningful in different types of communities from a sociolinguistic point of view, as explained in Formato and Somma (2023) and demonstrated in Safina's work.

---

[21] Pierucci (2021) suggests that the asterisk as an inclusive strategy was borrowed from IT language, where it is usually employed to indicate complex searches.

Facchini (2021) examined the use of the schwa in interpreting and found that different strategies were used depending on the complexity of the texts given to the twelve interpreters, including omission, neutral terms, generic feminines, and the schwa. In this work, there is also no mystification in that the schwa still seems not to be naturally engrained in the speech of these interpreters and generic masculines are described as still very much in use.

Starting from this, I here explore the phenomenon of the schwa on Twitter (now called X, following the change in ownership) through the following ideological stances: (a) speakers are to decide how to use language in its relation to gender identities and beliefs; (b) descriptive linguistics grants the opportunity to examine hues of usages that might escape intuitive understandings of language phenomena, as those discussed by some linguists; (c) communities are varied (see Formato and Somma, 2023).[22]

2.4 Examining Gender Inclusive Language in Italian

This section of this Element is dedicated to the analysis of schwa-words through corpus techniques and a novel approach to a corpus as an ethnographic site. This section is organised into themed subsections. I start by narrating the construction of the corpus and then explain how the corpus can be seen as an ethnographic site and the researcher as an ethnographer in digital space. The analysis follows and is divided into corpus-assisted results through quantitative patterns, examinations of how speakers *explain* the schwa through metalanguaging, and, finally, I present functions emerging from the digital ethnographic exploration of the corpus.

2.4.1 The Schwa-Corpus

To collect the corpus (and the sub-corpora), I decided against compiling or using a general corpus, instead focusing on a specific corpus of tweets which contained the schwa.[23] In CADS (and CL) jargon, this is referred to as a specialised corpus (Acarno, 2020; Gillings et al., 2023). In this specialised corpus, I see the tweets as 'texts' (Egbert and Schnur, 2018: 159) possessing three criteria: (i) naturally occurring – that is, genuine *speech*; (ii) recognisably

---

[22] In this Element, I use 'Twitter' and associated terms, rather than 'X', as the analysis was conducted before the change of the social media platform's name.

[23] In the general corpus of Italian ITtenten2020 (12,451,734,885 tokens, available through SketchEngine), research with *ə (* is here used as a wild card, allowing the collection of all occurrences of words ending in ə) produced an error, while searches with ə, produced 265 results, showing concordances of the schwa used as a phonetic symbol. This might be linked to the construction of the corpus. For similar reasons, Popič and Gorjanc (2018) decided against using a general corpus, as the phenomenon under investigation (underscore for gender inclusive Slovene) is of recent use.

self-contained – that is, language is cohesive as a unit and *proper* to the context/register in which it appears; and (iii) working functionally, where texts 'do not occur randomly or haphazardly. Rather they can be characterised by communicative functions that are intended by the author/speaker and interpretable by the reader/listener' (Egbert and Schnur, 2018: 162). This last point is paramount to collecting my data set, allowing the triangulation between CADS and FCDA to blossom. In order to have this specialised corpus, I decided to list some words which used the schwa on Twitter starting from observing four years (from 2019 to August 2022), using the advanced search on the social media and selecting fields 'word' (ə), 'language' (Italian) and 'dates' (2019, 2020, 2021, 2022). I compiled the list of words with two PhD students at the University of Brighton, Ashley Reilly Thornton and Chara Vlachaki, who were hired through the university's postgraduate research scheme. The criterion was to list all words appearing with the schwa (short and long) divided into years. Once the list was completed, I excluded adjectives (e.g., *rispettosə*/respectful, *inclusivə*/inclusive, *inglesə*/English, *oncologicə*/oncological), past participles (e.g., *andatə*/gone, *invitatə*/invited), and some nouns (e.g., *pazientə*/patient/s), in order to have a consistent corpus. I also noted that the long schwa was rarely used to indicate the plural, and the short schwa functioned for both singular and plural forms.

Furthermore, some speakers seemed to have used, yet not consistently, other orthographic signs to indicate the schwa, such as *3* (e.g., *inclusiv3*), perhaps due to the initial obstacle of not having the ə easily accessible on the Italian computer keyboards or that of the phone.[24] For this reason, my analysis does not include the use of *3* as an inclusive device. To obtain the corpus of the twenty-five schwa-words selected, I used *anaconda prompt* (iniconda3) in August 2022. Through a command, I requested the list of tweets, including the function (snscrape), the file format (jsonl), and the site where to scrape the words (twitter-search), followed by the terms in the list (Table 4). One crucial point is that I did not restrict the period under investigation, meaning that the scraper could capture all occurrences. The program created text files which contained each tweet and other information (what in corpus linguistics are usually called 'metadata'). I present an example in Figure 1, where some metadata elements have been replaced so that the tweet(er) could not be identified – for example, *url*.

In jsonl format, these files contain helpful information to *locate* the tweet (e.g., the date, the device, the number of followers of the person who tweeted, replies, quotes, etc.). I then used a downloadable program, OpenRefine, to

---

[24] Apple included the schwa in its keyboard in September 2021 (https://techgameworld.com/ios-15-introduces-the-schwa-for-more-inclusive-communication).

{"_type": "snscrape.modules.twitter.Tweet", "url": "*url*", "date": "*date*", "content": "*content*", "id": 1549787969095081985, "user": {"_type": "snscrape.modules.twitter.User", "username": "*user*", "id": 1480847902935244802, "displayname": "*displayname*", "description": "*description*", "rawDescription": "*description* lesbian", "descriptionUrls": null, "verified": false, "created": "date", "followersCount": number, "friendsCount": number, "statusesCount": number, "favouritesCount": number, "listedCount": 1, "mediaCount": 747, "location": "# ash", "protected": false, "linkUrl": "*link*", "linkTcourl": "*linktcourl*", "profileImageUrl": "*profile image*", "profileBannerUrl": "*profilebannerurl*", "label": null, "url": "url"}, "replyCount": number, "retweetCount": number, "likeCount": number, "quoteCount": number, "conversationId": 1549787969095081985, "lang": "it", "source": "<*source* rel=\"nofollow\">Twitter for *phone make*</a>", "sourceUrl": "*sourceUrl*", "sourceLabel": "Twitter for *phone make*", "outlinks": null, "tcooutlinks": null, "media": null, "retweetedTweet": null, "quotedTweet": null, "inReplyToTweetId": null, "inReplyToUser": null, "mentionedUsers": null, "coordinates": null, "place": null, "hashtags": null, "cashtags": null}

Figure 1 Example of Tweets and metadata provided by Anaconda

transform the jsonl files into Microsoft Excel files.[25] Open Refine allows for the extraction of a vast range of metadata among those available from the original files. For this study, I selected four elements, which descriptions (in Table 2) are borrowed from Di Cristofaro (2023: 192–8).

This metadata information, as well as the tweet (in the form of renderedContent), was useful to have some ideas about when the terms were used (date) and if specific hashtags could be useful in understanding the data set (hashtags.*). The files underwent cleaning, intending to investigate only genuine tweets written by the speakers rigorously, and the following were removed:

- Duplicates of tweets – for example, when speakers had sent the same tweet to different people.
- Tweets where the schwa-word was used in a language other than Italian – for example, carə (meaning *way/option* in Azerbaijani).
- Tweets where the schwa-word was the title of a newspaper/magazine article on the topic of inclusive language.
- Tweets where the schwa-word was not used as an inclusive strategy.

The Excel files produced were employed to familiarise with the data set, as in the CADS tradition, showing that no hashtag was consistently used. The list of

---

[25] https://openrefine.org.

Table 2 Metadata details used to collect the schwa-corpus

Attribute name	Type	Description
_type	string	Internal value added by snscrape, whose value describes the snscrape module used to collect the data (in the case of the Twitter search module, the value is snscrape. modules.twitter. Tweet)
Date	string	Date on which the tweet was posted, using the format YYYY-MM-DDTHH:MM:SS+TZ
hashtags.*	array	List of strings containing the hashtags included in the tweet's contents as strings stripped of the # character, one item for each hashtag
renderedContent	string	Content (from attribute content) of the tweet as it appears on the web or app interface and formatted without the use of the t.co URL shortener

Table 3 Schwa-words divided into categories

Categories	Words
Activism	*Compagnə* (comrade/s), *attivistə* (activist/s)
Kinship and friendship	*Ragazzinə/ragazzə* (young people), *nonnə* (grandparent/s), *figliə* (kid/s), *compagnə* (partner), *fidanzatə* (partner), *amicə* (friend/s)
Pronouns and adjectives	*tuttə* (all), *mieə* (my), *alcunə* (some), *carə* (dear)
School	*compagnə* (classmate/s), *alunnə* (student/s)
Work	*Colleghə* (colleague/s), *libraiə* (bookstore assistant/s), *proprietariə* (property owner/s), *autorə* (author/s), *scrittorə* (writer/s) *attorə* (actor/s), *psicologə* (psycologist/s), *disegnatorə* (designer/s), *dottorə*, *economistə*

terms selected (see Table 3) urged for some thinking to make the analysis viable and consistent, resulting in a categorisation of mainly semantic fields (*Activism, Kinship and friendship, School, Work*), but also one grammar-oriented field (*Pronouns and adjectives*).

This categorisation had to consider some semantic insights – for instance, the word *compagnə* has different meanings, and therefore its occurrences were split across the relevant categories: partner (in *Kinship and friendship*), comrades (in *Activism*), and schoolmates/university mates (in *School*).[26] Initially, the categories *School* and *Work* were put together; however, in familiarising myself with the sub-corpora, I noticed that the age (of the speakers) might be a factor worth considering. Specifically, younger users probably employ terms that refer to school or university more often than professional terms (e.g., *collegha*). While an apparent time approach – that is, selecting different age groups in the present to investigate linguistic change across years/periods and in the past (Bell, 2006) – is not the focus of this research, this could provide some interesting insights. In the category *Kinship and friendship*, *ragazza* and *ragazzina* have the same meaning: young people; however, the latter contains the suffix *–ina*, which usually adds the underlying sense of innocence (in positive and negative prosodies). In relation to what was suggested in Section 2.2 about the formation of the words, the terms *autora* (author/s), *scrittora* (writer/s), and *attora* (actor/s) appear on Twitter regardless of the criticisms concerning the masculine suffix (*tor–*). These are included in the category *Work*, which is the biggest in the number of terms (both in my corpus and in the words observed in the initial list). In Table 4, I report the number of occurrences for each word in the ad hoc Excel file, as part of the categories outlined previously in this Element, and the date on which the first tweet appeared in the schwa-form.

Note that this is not the final number of words for each of these terms, as occurrences of one term could also be found in other Excel files or used in association with other terms – for example, *miea amica* (my friends). Furthermore, the scraper found 32,836 occurrences of *tutta* (Eng. all/everybody, 6 occurrences in 2018, 10 in 2019, 440 in 2020, 12,030 in 2021, and 1,999 in the months of 2022 that I am investigating). Starting from this, I decided to extract a sample of 5,000 occurrences (2,000 from 2021 and 3,000 from 2022) based on an average of the other two high-frequency terms, *amica* (5,491) and *ragazza* (4,667). This corpus must be considered a sample in its methodological and theoretical implications. On this topic, Egbert and Schnur (2018) encourage researchers to establish an appropriate sampling unit based on the aims of the research but also to allow a solid investigation. Limitations and pitfalls are inevitable and are noted where they occur.

Similarly, it is undeniable that cherry-picking has occurred at different levels, as described by Baker (2018: 282), but attempts were made to build and examine the corpus consistently. In addition, some observations can be made – for instance, forms such as those included in the categories *Pronouns and adjectives* (6,786, only including a sample of *tutta*) and *Kinship and*

---

[26] Some occurrences did not belong to any of these three categories and were excluded from the analysis.

Table 4 Information (time and occurrences) about schwa-words

	Word	Dates	Occurrences in Excel files
Work	Attorə	04–2020	101
	Autorə	06–2020	216
	Colleghə	09–2020	269
	Disegnatorə	10–2020	5
	Dottorə	09–2020	52
	economistə	09–2020	6
	Libraiə	05–2020	19
	Proprietariə	10–2020	18
	Psicologə	08–2020	327
	Scrittorə	09–2020	51
Total			**1,064**
Activism	Attivistə	08–2020	395
	Compagnə	09–2020	362
Total			**757**
Pronouns and adjectives	Alcunə	07–2020	1,071
	Carə	08–2020	576
	tuttə	03–2018	5,000
	Mieə	09–2020	139
Total			**6,786**
Kinship and friendship	Amicə	06–2020	5,491
	Fidanzatə	08–2020	424
	Figliə	05–2011/ 10–2018	833
	Compagnə	01–2021	62
	Ragazzə	03–2019	4,667
	Ragazzinə	09–2020	277
	Nonnə	10–2020	47
Total			**11,801**
School	Alunnə	09–2020	81
	Compagnə	09–2020	157
Total			**238**
Overall total			**20,884**

friendship (11,801). These are the ones mostly rendered inclusive by Twitter users. These terms seem primarily used in informal and everyday language, descriptive of personal experiences. As in the CADS tradition, the corpus investigation is not solely based on frequency but rather on patterns originating from the corpus selected and with (possibly meaningful) low-frequency occurrences in sight (as in the serendipity explained in Section 1). In observing the dates on which these schwa-forms were first used, one can notice that most of them appeared on Twitter in the second part of 2020, possibly following the social media debate on the schwa. Only three terms were found to be used earlier – *figliə* (2018), *ragazzə* (2019), and *tuttə* (2018) – suggesting that some speakers were already renegotiating traditional and binary gendered morphemes. In Table 5, I present the number of tokens of the final corpus used for the investigation, referred to as the schwa-corpus, as well as the information about the sub-corpora referring to the five categories discussed earlier.

The corpora are different in size, and for this reason, statistical measures will be used in investigating frequency, collocations, and bigrams. The corpus tool used to investigate the corpora is Lancsbox 6.0 (Brezina, Weill-Tessier, and McEnery, 2020). Lancsbox is a free corpus tool for exploring languages, among which is Italian, also providing a tree tagger for parts of speech (POS). Before conducting the analysis, I checked how the tree tagger *reacted* to the schwa, as the assumption is that the tagger has been instructed to recognise the traditional binary morphemes. With the aim (or rather, hope) to investigate colligations – that is, '[a] form of collocation which involves relationships at the grammatical rather than the lexical level' (Baker, Hardie, and McEnery, 2006: 36), I conducted some queries to see how the words with the schwa were categorised. Possibly unsurprisingly, I noticed that there was no consistency in how these were tagged, as the following examples show:

Table 5 Number of tokens of the schwa-corpus and the categories of sub-corpora

Corpus	Number of tokens
Activism	22,705
Kinship and friendship	261,361
Pronouns and adjectives	148,256
School	7,250
Work	7,573
Schwa-corpus (and total)	**469,417**

- *Essə* was tagged as a noun and not as a pronoun.
- *Solə* was tagged as a noun and not as an adjective.
- *Colleghə* was tagged as an adjective and not as a noun.
- *Lə* was tagged as a noun and not as a determiner.

These examples raise methodological concerns as well as technological ones. I hope this Element and those following can initiate a discussion about how a tree tagger can account for inclusive forms, providing the same technological affordances used by those investigating noninclusive language.

2.4.2 The Corpus as an Ethnographic Site

In building and familiarising myself with the corpus and sub-corpora, I began to reflect on its relevance in social terms, offering ways for the researcher to connect with what the data set represents socially and politically. For these reasons, I here explore the idea that a corpus can be seen as an ethnographic site. Specifically, linguistic ethnography is based on 'reflexivity about the role of the researcher; attention to people's emic perspectives; sensitivity to in-depth understandings of particular settings; and openness to complexity, contradiction and re-interpretation over time' (Tusting, 2019: 1). Moreover, one of the directions of linguistic ethnography is digital ethnography, which is 'interested in ways in which people use language, interact with each other, employ discourses and construct communities, collectives, knowledge and identities through and influenced by digital technologies' (Varis and Hou, 2019: 230). These concepts lie in a solid foundation for discussing the following results, centring the ethnographic aspects around the corpus. Furthermore, the corpus is built from a digital platform, Twitter, a micro-blogging social media platform where public figures, institutions, media, and individuals exchange information. Twitter can be considered as a micro-context, with its own medium-related affordances (mentions, asymmetric following, and hashtags, referred to as social tags by Zappavigna (2017)), yet also intrinsically linked to and based on what happens, in terms of societal changes, outside the medium – that is, macro-contexts. The corpus compiled for this study is centred around a specific 'social' and linguistic event, in this case, the schwa, in what can be defined as an 'internet event' (Hine, 2000: 50). Similar to an ethnographer, I approached the social media platform Twitter to see *what is happening* in terms of linguistic behaviour, and especially *how*. The *how* is connected to Twitter as a place for the informal exchange of conversations, allowing relations to be forged. This social media site is also described as a semiotic technology (Zappavigna, 2017) in which the high level of possible interactivity is central. In this interactionality, exchange, and sharing, I conceive of my schwa-corpus as a digital ethnographic site where a range of activities, developing both in more traditional and offline traditional ethnographic research, happen. For instance, interactions occur through emojis, mentions, hashtags, and specific forms of community-building, as shown in the analysis. In digital ethnography, time is shifted (Varis and Hou, 2019) as the participants and the ethnographer do not have to be *there* simultaneously. In addition, time can be seen as a fruitful element in the in-depth understanding of the language (and cultural) phenomenon (as described in Section 2.4.1). The corpus thus becomes a specialised archive of how and when the linguistic phenomena occurred. To investigate language, I start from the understanding that 'social media are part of what can be characterised as the "messy web", resulting in an equally complex online ethnography process' (Postill and Pink, 2012: 126). With due differences to other ethnographic research, I am invisible to the speakers who used inclusive language, exploring linguistic actions in digital space and therefore a *register* (Twitter).

Moreover, I enter a space already inhabited by the language I investigate (see Section 2.1 for information). My aim is to *make sense* of some patterns having at their core the negotiation of traditional and novel gendered morphemes and, broadly, gender (as per investigation through FCDA). Seeing the corpus as an ethnographic site has been methodologically useful to split the analysis into several parts, some quantitative and based on aspects of frequencies (while also being complemented by qualitative insights), and others purely qualitative on metalanguaging and relevant functions of the schwa-words. Both investigations aim at providing a comprehensive picture of how gender inclusive language is used and the multiple functions it expresses on Twitter.

2.5 Gender Inclusive Language: What's in the Corpus?

In the following sections, I present the results of the investigation of gender-inclusive language from several perspectives. In Section 2.5.1, the results are based on investigating patterns through corpus techniques, and Section 2.5.2 examines metalanguaging of the linguistic phenomena, starting from a corpus-assisted examination. In Section 1, I explained the centrality of the corpus in CAD studies, and I here reiterate the importance of the term *assisted* in that 'corpus techniques are strictly functional to the overall task in hand' (Partington, 2006: 300). In Section 2.5.3, I show multiple functions of the schwa on Twitter, found through a digital ethnography of the corpus.

2.5.1 Corpus-Assisted Research of Gender-Inclusive Language: Quantitative Patterns

With the schwa-corpora at hand, I conducted a collocation analysis of *ə to explore words that statistically co-occur (referred to as collocates in CL) with those ending in the schwa. This allowed me to see whether the schwa was used in isolation or integrated into a more complex syntactical structure consisting of other inclusive terms. There have been criticisms that conceptualise Italian not as a versatile language for the many matching elements (also referred to as gender agreement) that would need changing to be made fully inclusive (see Section 2.3). For this reason, I have collected the collocates in plus two and minus two positions from the node; the rationale for this span is to explore proximate elements such as articles, adjectives, and nouns. Furthermore, tweets are usually brief texts and with the software not recognising sentence boundaries, the risk was that a longer span could capture textual elements from other tweets. The collocates were analysed for the six corpora (the schwa-corpus and each of the five sub-corpora). An MI3 score was used to examine the collocates' strength based on the observed and expected frequencies. In Table 6, I present the results, divided into the number of collocates with a schwa (for the first thirty words in each corpus), the percentages of the number of collocates that contained schwa-elements, whether noninclusive alternatives were present, and the number of the elements that could have been made inclusive but were not.

From the table, some interesting patterns emerge. Firstly, it shows that having sub-corpora is a good strategy for exploring insights into the distribution and how the schwa has the potential to work differently depending on the linguistic contexts. As can be noticed, the percentage of schwa-collocates ranges from 26.6 per cent for the corpus containing the adjective and pronoun forms to 36.6 per cent for the whole corpus and the *Kinship and friendship* category.

Table 6 Absolute frequencies and percentages of schwa-collocates

Corpus	Number of schwa-collocates	Percentage of schwa-collocates	Number of potentially noninclusive alternatives	Potential inclusive terms
Schwa	11/30	36.6%	0	0
Work	13/30	43.3%	0	0
Activism	14/30	46.6%	0	0
Pronouns and adjectives	8/30	26.6%	0	0
School	12/30	40.0%	1	0
Kinship and friendship	11/30	36.6%	2	2

The highest percentage of schwa-collocates can be found in the sub-corpora *School* (40 per cent), *Work* (43.3 per cent) and *Activism* (46.6 per cent). Possibly, the 46.6 per cent in the activism sub-corpus is not surprising because it consists of terms aimed at expressing forms of activism. Interestingly, in the sub-corpus *School*, there is one collocate which is not used inclusively, yet it is used as a split form (frequency: 7), somewhat indicating the intention of the speakers to avoid a generic term (usually masculine), as can be seen in:

(1) In bocca al lupo a **tuttə.INCL i/le.SPLIT miei/mie.SPLIT compagnə.INCL maturandə.INCL**, sopravvivremo anche a questo ✿ #maturita2021
     Good luck to all my schoolmates graduating, we will survive this too ✿ hashtag.

This sentence has a mix of inclusive elements – *tuttə, compagnə, maturandə* – and split forms that are masculine and feminine pairs (see Formato 2019) – that is, *i*.masc/*le*.fem (the), *miei*.masc/*mie*.fem (my).

In exploring the concordance lines of *un* and *del* in the *Kinship* sub-corpus, I found that, on some occasions (and therefore not statistically significant), they were used as (masculine) generics preceding schwa-words, as in (2):

(2) @mention ti dico la stessa cosa che ho detto a un.**MASC altrə.INCL ragazzə. INCL**: non so se tu faccia parte della comunità e non mi interessa saperlo, ma se tu non lo trovi irrispettoso non vuol dire che non lo sia dato che altre persone lo hanno trovato offensivo
     I repeat what I said to another young person: not sure if you are part of the community and I have no interest in knowing it, but if you do not find this disrespectful, that does not mean that other people cannot find it offensive.

In this example, the article used is in its masculine form but is followed by a schwa pair, possibly suggesting that some speakers prefer to emphasise some elements rather than others. However, one cannot exclude that speakers found it easier to recognise some elements that can be rendered inclusive and leave some others behind. The topic of articles or *preposizioni articolate* (i.e., preposition plus articles) is an interesting one, as also dealt with by Slemp et al. (2020) and Slemp (2021) when investigating tweets from Spanish. Their research found that speakers use inclusive language, either in the inclusive devices *–e* (*todes*) or *–x* (*todxs*), preceded by what they call 'doublets' (i.e., split forms, e.g., the articles *los*.masc/*las*.fem). These initial findings pushed me to investigate the co-occurrence phenomenon more closely. In order to do so, I conducted an n-gram analysis, choosing bigrams (i.e., exploring the frequencies of a sequence of two tokens) of schwa-words belonging to sub-corpora *Work*, *Activism*, *Kinship and friendship*, and *School* (see Table 4). The analytical framework has been built by manually investigating the bigrams. It explores not only the aforementioned articles and *preposizioni articolate* but also possessives (e.g., *nostr–*/our) and determiners (e.g., *quest–*, this/these), referred to as satellite elements. To summarise, these are the categorisations of the forms:

  i) **Inclusive forms**: for example, *deə* (of the), *ə* (the), *meə* (my), *questə* (this/these)
 ii) **Feminine forms**: for example, *delle* (of the), *le* (the), *mie* (my), *queste* (these)
iii) **Generic masculines**: for example, *del* (of the), *il* (the), *miei* (my), *questi* (these)
 iv) **Split forms**: for example, *del/le* (of the), *il/la* (the), *miei/mie* (my), *questi/queste* (these), whether they reproduce female firstness (first in the pair is the feminine) or male firstness (first in the pair is masculine)
  v) **Other forms**, for example, *di* (of)

Before explaining the results, I wish to explain some differences between feminine forms and generic masculines. As shown through the examples, it cannot be said that feminine forms are used as generics; they seem to be mismatching, or possibly deliberate use of feminine forms, when compared to the long tradition that has seen masculine forms used regardless of the gender of the referents.

The findings of these forms, divided for each schwa-word in the four sub-corpora, are presented in Table 7. In it, I present the absolute frequencies and percentages representing the relative frequency for each word and total within the sub-corpus and a comprehensive view of the sub-corpora in the final total row.

Starting from the results of each sub-corpus, I calculated the p-value to check whether these results had the probability of occurring randomly; using Pearson's Chi-squared test (a tool to measure categorical data), the results showed a p-value of 0.0001, demonstrating that these results are statistically significant. Table 7 provides interesting insights into how articles, *preposizioni articolate*, possessives, and determiners are used with the schwa-words investigated. Firstly, one notices that the total results show that the nouns are preceded by a wide range of inclusive devices (some of which are discussed qualitatively). Specifically, 80.71 per cent of forms are inclusive, showing the versatility and adaptability of forms aimed at achieving gender, or rather, inclusive gender agreement. All terms investigated have inclusive forms in their highest percentage compared to other types (i.e., feminine, masculine, and split forms). Masculine forms are, in the total results, those that follow (15.09 per cent), suggesting that rather than a simply masculine specificity, these still work as generics. This point needs more investigation as (in)consistencies construct interesting scenarios on possible biases about specific terms, as discussed later in this section. Split forms are the third highest used forms, with a small percentage (2.41 per cent). It is perhaps

Table 7 Absolute frequencies and percentages of satellite elements in their inclusive, feminine, masculine, and split forms

Term	Sub-corpus	Inclusive forms	Feminine forms	Masculine forms	Split forms	Total
attivista	Activism	83 (83.84%)	4 (4.04%)	9 (9.09%)	3 (3.03%)	99 (55.30%)
compagna		70 (87.5%)	2 (2.5%)	4 (5%)	4 (5%)	80 (44.69%)
Total Activism		153 (85.47%)	6 (3.35%)	15 (8.38%)	7 (3.91%)	179 (100%)
Ragazzina	Kinship and friendship	49 (70%)	0 (0%)	16 (22.86%)	5 (7.14%)	70 (3.05%)
Ragazze		476 (78.94%)	31 (5.14%)	78 (12.94%)	18 (2.99%)	603 (26.33%)
Nonna		13 (92.86%)	0 (0%)	1 (7.14%)	0 (0%)	14 (0.61%)
Figlie		421 (87.34%)	3 (0.62%)	54 (11.2%)	4 (0.83%)	482 (21.04%)
Compagne_Rel		32 (78.05%)	0 (0%)	7 (17.07%)	2 (4.88%)	41 (1.79%)
Fidanzate		140 (92.11%)	0 (0%)	6 (3.95%)	6 (3.95%)	152 (6.63%)
Amice		692 (74.57%)	9 (0.97%)	221 (23.81%)	6 (0.65%)	928 (40.52%)
Total Kinship and friendship		1,823 (79.61%)	43 (1.88%)	383 (16.72%)	41 (1.79%)	2,290 (100%)
Compagne_Sch	School	45 (76.27%)	1 (1.69%)	5 (8.47%)	8 (13.56%)	59 (67.81%)
Alunne		19 (67.86%)	0 (0%)	5 (17.86%)	4 (14.29%)	28 (32.18%)
Total School		64 (73.56%)	1 (1.15%)	10 (11.49%)	12 (13.79%)	87 (100%)
Colleghe	Work	3 (27.27%)	2 (18.18%)	3 (27.27%)	3 (27.27%)	11 (3.15%)
Libraie		7 (100%)	0 (0%)	0 (0%)	0 (0%)	7 (2%)
Proprietarie		6 (54.55%)	0 (0%)	4 (36.36%)	1 (9.09%)	11 (3.15%)

Autore	34 (75.56%)	0 (0%)	9 (20%)	0 (0%)	45 (12.89%)
Scrittore	16 (88.89%)	0 (0%)	1 (5.56%)	1 (5.56%)	18 (5.15%)
Psicologo	224 (95.73%)	0 (0%)	6 (2.56%)	4 (1.71%)	234 (67.04%)
Disegnatore	3 (75%)	0 (0%)	1 (25%)	0 (0%)	4 4 (1.14%)
Dottore	8 (47.06%)	0 (0%)	8 (47.06%)	1 (5.88%)	17 (4.87%)
economista	2 (100%)	0 (0%)	0 (0%)	0 (0%)	2 (0.57%)
Total *Work*	303 (86.82%)	2 (0.57%)	32 (9.17%)	10 (2.87%)	349 (100%)
Total	**2,343 (80.71%)**	**52 (1.79%)**	**438 (15.09%)**	**70 (2.41%)**	**2,903 (100%)**

Table 8 Inclusive forms used in the corpus and traditional binary forms

Grammatical category	Inclusive forms	*Traditional* binary forms (fem.sing/fem.plur/ masc.sing/masc.plur)	Translation into English
Articles	ə, lə	La, lo, il	Singular the
	glə, ə	Le, gli, i	Plural the
	unə, un3, unx	Una, un', uno, un	a/an
Preposizioni articolate	dellə, deə, delə, deglə	Della, dello, delle, degli, dei	Of the
	daə, də	Dalla, dallo, dalle, dagli, dai	From the
	allə, aə, alə	Alla, allo, alle, agli, ai	At the/to the
	sullə	Sulla, sullo, sulle, sugli, sui	On the
	nelə	Nella, nello, nelle, negli, nei	In the
Possessives	nostrə, mieə, miə, suə, tuə, tuoə,	Mia, mio, mie, miei	My
	vostrə, miaə, mieiə, suoə	Tua, tuo, tue, tuoi	Your
		Sua, suo, sue, suoi	His/Her/Their (singular)
		Nostra, nostro, nostre, nostri	Our
		Vostra, vostro, vostre, vostri	Your
Determiners	stə, queə, quelə, questə, quelə	Questa, questo, queste, questi	This/these
		Quella, quello, quelle, quegli, quei	That/those

unsurprising that the speakers do not prefer these as they reproduce the binary masculine/feminine (and, with regard to social gender, male and female) and, therefore, they might be seen as hindering the goal of inclusivity. This can be possibly used as a counterargument to Russell's (2024) scepticism about the possible binarism of gender inclusive forms. Here the speakers seem to understand what is binary and what goes beyond it. There are no cases of split forms that include inclusive forms too – for instance, *il/la/lə* (or other inclusive forms), and all split forms are gender binary. In addition to this, the split pairs appear in male firstness – that is, as Baker (2013) suggests, when the masculine form precedes the feminine: *gli/le* or *i/le* (plural the), *dei/lle* (of the), *il/la* (singular the), *mio/mia* (my), *suoi/e* (his/her), *un/a* (a), *quei/quelli* (those) and *sugli/sulle* (on the). Female firstness is seen in the pairs *alle/agli* (at the/to the), *la/il* (singular the), and *le/gli* (plural the). In examining the total findings, the lowest percentage is that of feminine forms, with 1.79 per cent. Starting from this, I explain some interesting uses of these forms in the following paragraphs. In relation to inclusive forms, I present Table 8 to show the different forms employed in the tweets.

Previously, I mentioned that inclusive forms are the ones that are mostly used in the corpora. I find this to be an important insight into how speakers find inclusive solutions for gender agreement, as issues around syntactical functioning have always been among the fiercest criticism among linguists (as in Arcangeli's petition, see Section 2.3) and other speakers. For this reason, I see articles and *preposizioni articolate* as the speakers' battle fought on the ground, pushing forward ways in which inclusive language can be fully used. As for articles (the English *the*), the ə is used in the singular and the plural forms, while other solutions are used together with existing articles – that is: (1) *glə* replacing masculine plural *gli*, thus highlighting the efforts made to avoid generic masculines yet drawing from them to create inclusive forms; (2) *lə*, which resembles the feminine *la* and the masculine *lo*, in their singular forms. The indefinite article (the English *a/an*) is used with three inclusive devices that are the short schwa *unə*, the ɜ possibly replacing the long schwa (ɜ), as per Boschetto's recommendations (see Section 2.3), *un3*, and the morpheme *x* (see Table 1), *unx*. When we look at the *preposizioni articolate* (of, at, to, on, in + articles), it can be seen that the schwa, in most cases, replaces the gendered morpheme traditionally used in similar feminine and masculine forms. It might be that the speakers see *dell–* (of the), *all–* (from the) or *sull–* (on the) as general forms, as they are used with singular and plural gendered morphemes. An example of this is *della* (feminine.sing), *dello* (masculine.sing), and *delle* (feminine.plur) replaced by *dellə*, also encapsulating *degli* (masculine.plur), as in (3):

(3) Sono terrorizzata.**FEM** dalle decisioni che vengono prese per noi e per le future generazioni dietro le porte chiuse dei palazzi istituzionali. Sul futuro nostro e su quello **dellǝ.INCL nostrǝ.INCL figliǝ.INCL** pende la spada di Damocle della negligenza istituzionale di fronte alla crisi ecologica.

I am terrified by the decisions made for us and for future generations behind the closed doors of institutional buildings. The sword of Damocles, the institutional negligence in dealing with the ecologic crisis, hangs over our future and that of our children.

In (3), there is agreement among the three elements: the *preposizione articolata*, the possessive, and the noun, with the solution of *dell–* plus the schwa. Other prepositions have the same type of inclusive forms – for example, *allǝ, sullǝ*, as in (4) and (5):

(4) Sostegno **allǝ.INCL attivistǝ.INCL** che si mobilitano oggi, nella giornata mondiale dell'acqua, contro la Gigafactory Tesla a Berlino/Brandenburg!

(Let's) Support the activists mobilising today, on World Water Day, against the Tesla Gigafactory in Berlin/Brandenburg!

(5) Tra i luoghi comuni **sullǝ.INCL attivistǝ.INCL**, uno è particolarmente duro a morire: quello dei.**MASC** giovani.**EPIC**. 'Ci pensano i.**MASC** giovani.**EPIC**', 'i.**MASC** giovani.**EPIC** per il clima', 'la battaglia dei.**MASC** giovani.**EPIC**' sono frasi che i media ripetono in continuazione.

In the common myths about activists, one is hard to die: that of young people. 'Young people will think about it', 'the young people's support for the climate', 'the battle of young people': media are constantly repeating sentences like these.

However, the investigation of the corpora also shows other types of inclusive forms – for instance, *alǝ* (to/at the), *delǝ* (of the), and *nelǝ* (in the), signalling the efforts of the speakers in avoiding the double *ll* as that would only cover three out of the five options for the preposition (e.g., *dello, della, delle, degli, dei*). Example (6) appears as part of a thread (i.e., a chain of tweets) of an association interested in the rights of those who write comics:

(6) … le prospettive future e le attività di MeFu, ovviamente e necessariamente dal punto di vista **delǝ.INCL autorǝ.INCL**.

The future work and the activity of MeFu, are seen through the lens of the authors.

Another option employed is the preposition plus the schwa, although it only appears for two prepositions, *daǝ* (from the) and *aǝ* (at/to the). 'From the' is also used in the form *dǝ*, possibly a more confusing option as it could be both *da* (from) or *di* (of), only left to the context to be disambiguated. With reference to the plural form, some other speakers choose to modify the masculine form, using *deglǝ*, stemming from *degli*, as in (7):

(7) Comincio a rendermi conto che i consigli sono il MALE e capisco anche perché
non è compito **deglǝ.INCL psicologǝ.INCL** darne.
I begin to realise that giving advice is BAD and I understand why it's not the
therapist's task to provide it.

Similar to the variety of options for the prepositions, the possessives and the
determiners appear in various forms in the corpus. The determiners seem to
follow what happens for the articles, with forms that replace the double *ll* with
one *l* – for example, *quelǝ* – or the use of the double *ll* – for example, *quellǝ*
(both translated into English as that/those). Some remove the consonant group
and use the root *que–* plus the schwa – for example, *queǝ* – while the English
'this/that/these/those' sees the replacement of the gendered morphemes with
a schwa in its complete form and shortened versions, *questǝ* and *stǝ* respectively. Regarding possessives, while speakers do not have problems replacing
the gendered binary morphemes with a schwa when there is only one root – for
example, *nostrǝ, vostrǝ* – more flexibility is found for other persons. For
instance, the first person is used in the forms *mieǝ* and *mieiǝ* (stemming from
miei, the masculine plural), where the latter can be a(n involuntary) typo in
writing inclusive from the habitual masculine generic; *suoǝ* and *tuoǝ*, originating from the masculine plural *tuoi* and *suoi* are also used in the same way. In
addition to these forms, some speakers used *miǝ/tuǝ/suǝ*, resembling the feminine plural *mie, tue, sue*. These results call for a reflection on standardisation as
a general term and, more specifically, with regard to the schwa-forms.

One can see that these go beyond the recommendations made by Gheno
(2022) and Boschetto, portraying a more complex scenario in which, perhaps,
speakers are experimenting beyond the *said* and *known*. For instance, Facchini
(2021) found that using the schwa was not always linear in investigating
interpreters. In addition, the multiple forms are not to be seen, as anti-schwa
linguists believe, as a weakness. On the contrary, it shows that if these forms are
to empower speakers in their relations with themselves and others, then the
speakers themselves are to keep control of the linguistic experiment(ation)
outside a (recommended) regulatory frame. In other words, speakers engage
in (linguistic) identity work and negotiate what they know regarding grammatical gender and how these can be made inclusive. This proves that the idea of
languagers and languaging and, in this specific case, genderers and gendering, is
central. Genderers, in negotiating inclusive language, are embedding ideas
about the *standard*, which swings between generic masculines and binary
forms, and its rejection. As many studies have demonstrated in the past, the
standard should not be considered neutral and part of a balanced system, as
masculines have for two long considered generics in contrast with the grammatical system containing feminine and masculine morphemes. Therefore, the

speakers' efforts are paramount to understanding how society is changing and how language connects with this. This also raises another important point, as discussed by Banegas and Lopez (2021) regarding gender inclusive forms, that of normalisation within language change. The tweets investigated earlier suggest that schwa-forms are used competently from the speakers' point of view (pending mistakes or mismatches), and to some extent, one can suggest that the schwa does not create misunderstandings and is used *naturally*; however, this cannot be seen exclusively through the lens of the speakers, as readers could also be interrogated about *naturality* in the exchange. I believe the written register of the tweets is an advantage, as those who interact with the schwa-forms might have a chance to reread or become accustomed to the new forms. The *reading* is not neutral, as some speakers might reject these forms and believe they hinder mutual intelligibility, as Calder (2022) explained through the cislingual perspective adopted by some hearers.

Furthermore, the symbolic political values of grammatical gender and language inclusivity do not exempt from language as a political tool, specifically for far-right parties (see Borba, 2019; 2022). The tweet that follows does not belong to the corpus; however, it contributes to explaining the scenario in which the schwa appears. Members of far-right parties Fratelli d'Italia and Lega have been observed speaking against inclusive language or mocking it, as in the tweet of former senator Simone Pillon.[27] In commenting on the new leader of the PD, the first woman in the role, he writes:

> **Lə.INCL** *nuovə.***INCL** *segretariə.***INCL** *#Shlein è cittadin*.***INCL** **american*.INCL** *di orgini* **svizzer*.INCL**. *Un verso* **commissariə.INCL** *di Davos,* **rampollə.INCL** *radical chic,* **incaricatə.INCL** *del grande reset, cominciando da gender, aborto, agenda LGBT e quant'altro. Ora voglio capire come faranno i cattolici a continuare a votare #PD*

> The new leader is an American citizen of Swiss origins. A real spokesperson of Davos, a radical chic scion, in charge of the big reset, starting from gender, abortions, LGBT agenda and more. It escapes me how Catholics will vote for the Partito Democratico.

I see this in connection with far-right parties defending national borders from foreign threats and, similarly, limiting language. Examples such as these can be traced in the sense of nostalgia for a mythical past, as described in Section 1, triggering what are defined as linguistic guerrilla wars (Cameron, 1995; Borba, 2019), as well as constructing moral panic (as explained in Section 1). I now move to discuss feminine and masculine forms as some telling insights show the complexity of *thinking* inclusive and the various

---

[27] https://twitter.com/SimoPillon/status/1630298853286051845.

degrees for it. If we explore the sub-corpora, we see that masculine forms are the second preferred form. An exception is the sub-corpus *School*, where masculine forms ranked third (11.49 per cent), preceded by split forms (13.79 per cent); in the sub-corpus *Kinship and friendship*, feminine forms, which are usually the least used, appear slightly more used (1.88 per cent) than split forms (1.79 per cent).

The differences are minimal; however, some patterns captured my attention and can be seen as serendipity (see Section 1). For instance, in the sub-corpus *Kinship and friendship*, the terms *ragazzinə* and *ragazzə*, referring to adolescents or young people, behave differently in relation to articles, *preposizioni articolate*, possessives and determiners. In exploring the concordances of *ragazzinə*, it can be noted that no feminine forms are employed. At the same time, it is different for *ragazzə*, possibly hinting at the idea that *ragazzə* is perceived through a female lens more than *ragazzinə*, which, in turn, might be seen as a generic. The two terms are mostly used with inclusive forms (70 per cent for *ragazzinə* and 78.94 per cent for *ragazzə*) and masculine forms (22.86 per cent and 12.94 per cent, respectively). In the same sub-corpus, two other schwa-words stand out: *figliə* (daughter/s – son/s – offspring/s) and *amicə* (friend/s), because they are preceded by masculine forms (11.2 per cent and 23.81 per cent, respectively) as their second preferred choice. Feminine and split forms are numerically distant from the masculine form (feminine: 0.62 per cent for *figliə* and 0.97 per cent for *amicə*; split forms: 0.83 per cent and 0.65 per cent, respectively). The plausible explanations concern a cultural bias, perhaps mostly for *figliə*; Italian is one of those cultures with a legacy of a hierarchy where baby boys used to have a better cultural value than baby girls (see Formato, 2019). The masculine forms for *amicə* could depend on the schwa-word, as it is used with the masculine plural root (*amic–*, also the root for feminine and masculine singular) rather than the feminine plural root (*amich–*). In the sub-corpus *school*, the terms *compagnə* (schoolmates) and *alunnə* (students/pupils) also behave differently. Both are preceded mostly by inclusive forms (76.27 per cent and 67.86 per cent); however, *compagnə* is preceded, in order, by split forms (13.56 per cent), masculine forms (8.47 per cent) and feminine forms (1.69 per cent, only one occurrence). In comparison, *alunnə* is preceded by masculine forms (17.86 per cent), split forms (14.29 per cent) and no feminine ones. With such small numbers, it is difficult to provide any solid explanation about preferences; however, I believe that some trends can be seen from the concordances shown in Figures 2 and 3.

From these concordances, it seems that, unsurprisingly, *compagnə* is mostly used for high schools/university and from the perspective of the

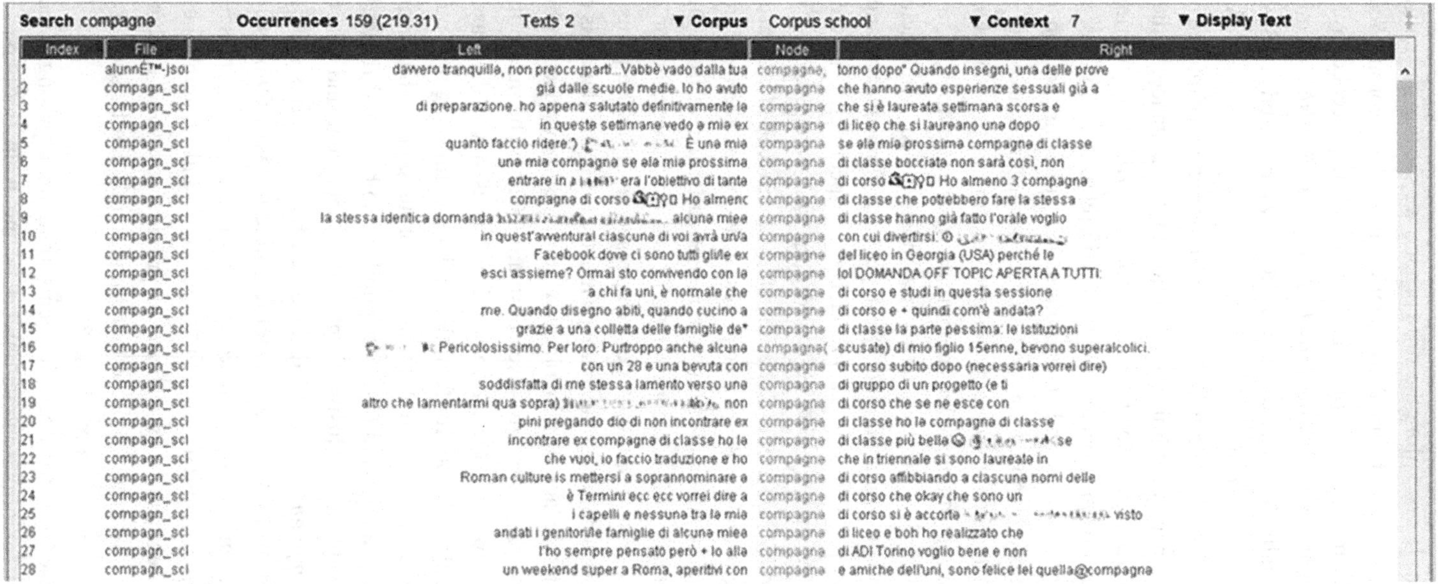

Figure 2 Concordances of *compagne* (sub-corpus *school*)

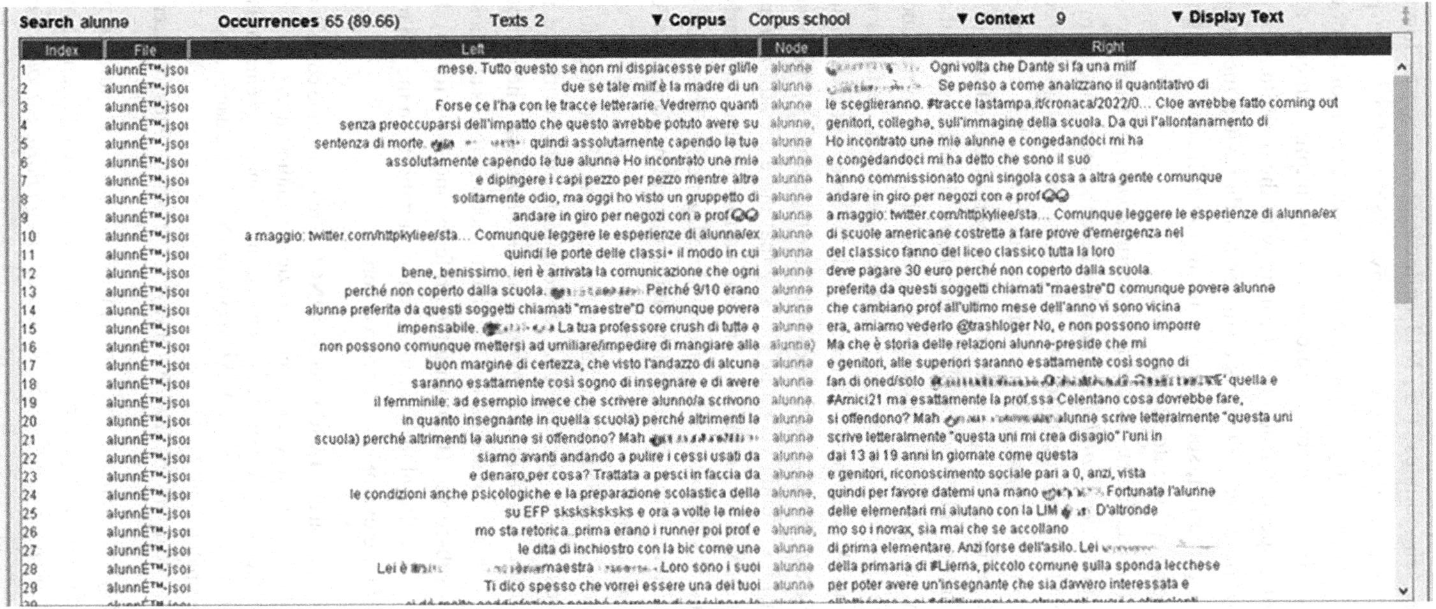

Figure 3 Concordances of alunnə (sub-corpus *school*)

'I plus my schoolmates' (–2, MI3 collocates: *mie*/my, *ex*/former, *alcune*/some, in the pair *alcune* plus possessive, *lə*/the, also in the pair *lə* plus possessive). Differently, *alunnə* is a more general term for other educational institutions. It is used by people describing pupils/students as a generic category or a specific group (collocating with the definite article *lə* and the indefinite article *unə*). There is a suggestion that when inclusive forms are not used or preferred, some generic terms are still seen through the lens of 'male as norm' (Formato, 2019).

Different trends can be noticed for the term *compagnə* in a relationship (partner/sub-corpus *Kinship and friendships*), where the masculine form is second in preference (17.07 per cent) followed by split forms (4.88 per cent) and no feminine forms; *Compagnə* in the sub-corpus *School* has as second preferred option split forms (13.56 per cent), followed by masculine forms (8.47 per cent) and feminine ones (1.69 per cent). A different trend can be seen in the sub-corpus *Activism* when *compagnə* means comrades, the split forms and masculine forms have the same percentage (5 per cent), and female forms are used too (2.5 per cent). Among these differences, and if we move past the main preference for the inclusive forms, what stands out is the higher use of the masculine form in relationships. Tentatively, one can say that there are still reminiscences of heteronormativity when the word means partner or that, similarly to *alunnə* (sub-corpus *School*), this term is considered generic. This shows that there could be different options regarding using masculine forms that can be seen through a social lens.

In addition, it can be noticed that feminine forms are not used for most of the schwa-words, except for *colleghə* (colleagues). Split forms are not used in relation to *libraiə*, *autorə*, *disegnatorə*, and *economistə*. The numbers are very small here; however, it seems striking that masculine forms are those employed in the *Work* sub-corpus (following the preferred inclusive forms). I argue here that a legacy of cultural ideas around gender suitability in the job market could still *hover*. Some examples are offered here:

(8) Io ho bisogno di un.**MASC psicologə.INCL** perché mi rendo conto di non essere in grado di gestire in maniera corretta emozioni e sentimenti
I need a therapist because I realise that I cannot manage my emotions and feelings.

(9) @mention Ma poi perché i.**MASC scrittorə.INCL** etero danno ai personaggi queer sempre finali tragici??
Also why do heterosexual writers always resort to tragic ends for queer characters??

In (8) and (9), we see masculine forms in both singular and plural forms, showing that, in some cases, efforts to write inclusively are accompanied by old sexist practices. For some words, such as *autorə*, *disegnatorə*, *psicologə, and dottorə*, the inclusive forms originate from masculine roots (*autore, disegnatore, psicologo/psicologi*, and *dottore*, feminine forms are *autrice, disegnatrice, psicologa/psicologhe, dottoressa*, see Section 2.2). Therefore, it is likely that the visible masculine roots for these are still shaping preferences for articles, *preposizioni articolate*, determiners, and possessives in masculine forms.

To conclude, the analysis of these forms has shown the complexity and flexibility of choices. It has allowed for an in-depth examination of the dynamicity of speakers in building themselves and others through these new forms.

2.5.2 Metalanguaging: Allyship and Rejection

To explore how speakers conceptualise the schwa in sociolinguistic terms, I conducted a corpus-assisted search, searching 'schwa' in the schwa-corpus (fifty-three occurrences). I found it interesting how speakers talk about the schwa, which I refer to as metalanguaging, rather than attitudes towards gender inclusive language. The investigation that follows is, precisely, not a systematic attitude study, as the tweets used to provide an overview originate from a corpus-assisted ethnographic work on the corpus. Studies that investigate attitudes are prolific in several languages (e.g., Bonnin and Coronel (2021) and Slemp et al. (2020) for Spanish, Nodari (2022) for Italian, Renström et al. (2022) for Swedish, and Hekanaho (2022) for English) and ad hoc conferences have paid attention to these (e.g., *Attitudes towards gender-inclusive language: A multinational perspective*, 8–9 September 2022 (an online conference), and *Gender-neutral / fair / inclusive / non-binary / non-sexist languages and their dis/contents*, 16–17 October 2023, University of Chicago Center in Paris).[28] Interconnections can be seen between speakers, politics, and gender-inclusive language emphasising the political nature of this linguistic phenomenon. I also covered the debate around novelty and nostalgia, stemming from initial findings from this book, in my talk at Lavender 29 (titled *Nostalgia vs novelty: Speakers' choices resolving criticism towards inclusive language*). Moving away from attitudes, Jaworski, Coupland, and Galasinski (2012) argue that the process of metalanguaging is complex as it touches on several aspects of how communicators refer to, explain, and comment on their talk or that of others. Metalanguage is related to marking 'personal or group identities' (Jaworski et al., 2012: 4) and is involved in personal identification work as well as social relationship work. Language is contextualised and explained through representation and evaluation; because of this, metalanguage enters 'public

---

[28] www.qmul.ac.uk/sllf/linguistics/research/gender-inclusive-language/conference-attitudes-towards-gender-inclusive-language.

consciousness' (Jaworski et al., 2012: 3) and works at ideological levels. In other words, commenting on language is social work. Furthermore, meta-languaging can be associated with the wide debate on speakers (linguists and not) meddling with language through evaluative stances, an aspect that is prominent in the work of Cameron (1995), the so-called verbal hygiene. In accounting for the space restrictions of this Element, verbal hygiene relates to many aspects of normativity (in relation to grammatical rules), ideology (in relation to linguistic change), social practices (in relationships among speakers), cultural and political significance, and personal linguistic histories (in relation to identity but also agency).

One of the most interesting aspects is allyship and how this is visible through the use of the schwa or talking about the schwa. To investigate allyship, I argue that it appears in indirect and direct forms. The indirect one is described in Sections 2.5.1 and 2.5.2 – that is, using the schwa as a gender inclusive device in nouns and other gendered elements. In my view, direct allyship is when the speaker openly defends and stands by inclusive linguistic devices (the schwa and others). In the following examples, I present some concordances (10) – (14) of direct allyship, each providing nuances in the relationship between the linguistic event and the speaker's ideas and beliefs around the topic:

(10) @mention si usa per riferirsi a tutti.**MASC**. invece di dire appunto 'tutti' si dice **tuttə.INCL**. ad esempio ciao a **tuttə.INCL, qualcunə.INCL, ragazzə.INCL** ecc
@mention it is used to refer to everybody, instead of saying, precisely 'everybody', one can say everybody, for instance ciao all, someone, youngsters, etc.

(11) @mention @mention @mention Dottoressa.**FEM** è il femminile. Dottore.**MASC** se ti riferisci a un uomo, dottoressa.**FEM** ad una donna, **dottorə.INCL** se ti riferisci a un gruppo di uomini e donne o a una persona non binaria. Questa è l'idea dietro allo schwa.
Dottoressa is feminine. Dottore if you refer to a man, dottoressa to a woman, **dottorə.INCL** if you refer to a group of men and women or to a non-binary person. This is the idea behind the schwa.

(12) @mention Allora io lotto ogni cazzo di giorno così come **lə.INCL** mie.**FEM com-pagnə.INCL**. Da anni. A te non serve la schwa perché non sei una soggettività esclusa. Serve TUTTO. Una cosa non esclude l'altra. Se non la vuoi usare non la usi, ma per **moltə.INCL** è un passo importantissimo.
So, I have been fucking fighting every single day as much as my comrades. For a long time. You do not need (to use) the schwa as you are not excluded as an individual. Everything is needed. One aspect does not exclude the other. If you do not want to use it, don't but for many, this is a very important step.

(13) avevo già iniziato ad usare lo schwa quando ci scrivevamo, e nei vocali evitavo di usare aggettivi riferiti alla sua persona per non declinarli al maschile o al femminile.
I had already started to use the schwa when we were writing to each other and in audio messages to avoid using feminine or masculine adjectives.

(14) nb: nel thread ho usato la schwa per parlare di lesbiche perché he/him e they/them lesbians esistono e in particolare **alcunə.INCL miə.INCL** mutuals **lesbichə.INCL** usano i pronomi they/them e non voglio rischiare di dare fastidio a **qualcunə.INCL**, vi prego di fare lo stesso.

Please note: in the thread I used the schwa to talk about lesbians because he/him and they/them lesbians exist and specifically some of my mutual lesbians use the they/them pronoun and I do not want to upset anyone, so I ask you to do the same.

In (10) and (11), the speakers suggest how the schwa should be used and who it refers to, offering some examples. In (12), the tweet is an answer to someone who is more likely opposing the use of the schwa (the original tweet was deleted); the speaker fiercely explains how the schwa resolves the feeling of exclusion in society and language, reproducing empathy (Kolek, 2022). Whether or not the speaker forms part of this group, as it remains unclear from the tweet, the allyship is seen in the alignment to the schwa as a symbolic resource for many (*per moltə*). In connection with the public debate, this is an interesting and telling point as it explains the political force embedded in the morpheme, contrasting those views that see the schwa as an imposition. Rather, we see in these examples and in others in this section that gender inclusive language can be seen as a site of advocacy (Konnelly et al., 2022). In my view, the discourse of feeling compelled to use this device is used purposefully and politically to reject ideas around inclusive language and gender, fuelling moral panic. In (13), we see a speaker explaining their choices with respect to a specific individual. This tweet can be seen through the notion of outgroup-focused motivation, the desire to improve the condition of a discriminated and disadvantaged group (Radke et al., 2020), in which one's own privilege is recognised. Similarly, in (14), an elaboration of how the schwa is doing allyship work for a specific group of people, some of whom are in the speaker's social circle. Differently from (12), example (14) shows the speaker asking for collaboration on how to represent other people linguistically, inviting a reflection on respect (*vi prego di fare lo stesso*/I ask you to do the same), which can be seen as a moral motivation (Radke et al. 2020). For them, morality is based on an identification with a superordinate group and action is prompted by the recognition of the disadvantages suffered by the group. From the same perspective, in (15), there is a positive message in relation to the schwa:

(15) Comunque ho letto più post con la schwa in queste 24 ore che nei 24 mesi precedenti. E appena sarà presente come carattere in tutte le tastiere la vedremo crescere esponenzialmente. Perché le idee non si fermano, **ragazzə.INCL**

I read more posts with the schwa in the last 24 hours than in the previous 24 months. And as soon as it will be available on keyboards, we will see it exponentially more. Because we cannot stop ideas (from blossoming), folks.

No clues can help categorise allyship work, as this seems a more general statement about the observed use of the schwa. However, reading the speaker's alignment with the cause is possible. Similarly, speakers are also willing to engage in sociolinguistic discussion of the phenomenon through a positive lens as, for instance, in (16):

(16) @mention esiste anche la schwa [ə] (al plurale [ɜ]) che si pronuncia come la fine delle parole in napoletano! è neutro e perfettamente pronunciabile, e si usa così: oggi sono **andatə.INCL** a fare la spesa con **lə.INCL miə.INCL** migliore **amicə.INCL.** poi siamo **andatɜ.INCL** al parco. ci siamo **divertitɜ. INCL** tantissimo!

@mention there is also the schwa [ə] (plural [ɜ]) that is pronounced like the ending in some Neapolitan words! It is neuter, perfectly pronounceable, and used as follows: Today I went shopping with my best friends. Then we went to the park. We enjoyed it a lot!

This tweet is sent in response to a thread that deals with non-binary linguistic preferences, where information about personal subject pronouns is also shared. Similar to the other cases discussed in Section 2.5.1, the speaker here explains how the schwa can be flexible when matching all elements in the sentence, following Boschetto's recommendations on the use of the long schwa. The reference to the Neapolitan dialect is useful for understanding the Italian context and is employed to explain how this sound is not alien or foreign. In Section 2.3, I suggested that, conversely, linguists and the general audience use this geographical-oriented argument to demonise both the Neapolitan dialect and the gender inclusive schwa. More specifically, in the change.org petition, the linguist Arcangeli writes that the schwa is *peculiare di diversi dialetti italiani, . . ., stante la limitazione posta al suo utilizzo (la posizione finale), trasformerebbe l'intera penisola, se lo adottassimo, in una terra di mezzo compresa pressappoco fra l'Abruzzo, il Lazio meridionale e il calabrese dell'area di Cosenza* (is specific to several Italian dialects, . . ., in its limited use as the ending of a word, if we had to adopt it would turn the whole peninsula in a middle earth in between Abruzzo, the low Lazio and the Calabria area of Cosenza).[29] This linguist describes an area that is bigger than where Neapolitan is thought to be spoken, including the low Lazio, the region bordering Campania in the north, Abruzzo (bordering Lazio from the west) and Calabria, which is South of Campania. In his argument, there seems to be more than a neutral geographical description of the sound schwa. I believe that a discriminatory attitude towards these southern areas can be read through the lines. It is not novel to find discrimination with reference to

---

[29] www.change.org/p/lo-schwa-%C9%99-no-grazie-pro-lingua-nostra.

southern dialects, stemming from a broader and long-term social discrimination based on stereotypes about education, engagement with the state, and criminality (mafia) (Mioni and Arnuzzo-Lanszweert, 1979).[30] The north–south divide is historical and goes back to the unification of Italy in 1861. Furthermore, in (16), there is also what I believe is an interesting argument: the idea of the schwa being neuter. In this Element, I have widely discussed that terms such as 'neutralisation', 'neuter', and 'neutral' are possibly a disservice to what gender-inclusive language *does*, which is not to cancel, erase, and neutralise gender. It does the opposite, in my view, as it makes gender visible and political. It, specifically, *tells* hearers about discrimination, injustice, and the different future one wishes or expects; it is part, in other words, of the construction of a more welcoming society. In terms of linguistic realisations, speakers who are allies seem to have clear what is still central to the debate of both gendered and gender inclusive language, as shown in (17):

(17) Il problema non è lo schwa, la difficoltà nel pronunciarlo, 'l'inesistenza in italiano'(?) o l'Accademia della Crusca che non vuole. Il punto è che il maschile sovraesteso piace perché – secondo **alcunə.INCL** – i ruoli di decisione devono essere ricoperti da uomini.

The schwa is not the problem, the trouble in pronouncing it, 'the nonexistence in Italian'(?) or the academy of La Crusca that does not want it. The point is that the generic masculine is liked because – according to some – men must hold decision-making roles.

Here, we see how speakers conceptualise the schwa regarding broad ideas about language and society, foregrounding a mystification put forward by those who reject this inclusive device. Genderers are, therefore, moving within a space where there is a constant renegotiation of linguistic forms, where they acknowledge that sexist generic masculines continue to exist and be meaningful in a male-oriented society (Formato, forthcoming).

Through these examples, we have seen how direct allyship can raise awareness of language functioning, highlighting activisms by individuals helping shape the debate in several ways. Allyship also needs to be seen in relation to its counterargument – that is, the firm rejection of these forms. For instance, some resort to the *known* explanation that *there are more important things* than language (see Formato, 2019; Vergoossen, Pärnamets, Renström, and Gustafsson Sendén, 2020), as shown in (18):

---

[30] Or southern people, especially after the war when many moved to the North to work, as in the work of H. Merrill (2011). Migration and surplus populations: Race and deindustrialization in northern Italy. *Antipode*, 43(5), 1542–72.

(18) @mention @mention Ma secondo voi davvero studentesse.**FEM** e **operaiə.INCL**, docenti.**EPIC** e **attivistə.INCL** discutono insieme da anni nelle assemblee dello schwa? Ma voi davvero fate?
　　Do you really think that students, factory workers, teachers, and activists debate the schwa in their meetings? Are you for real?

While not directly showing why the schwa is an unsuitable solution, this tweet narrates a specific story concerning job roles or activism. More specifically, it can be seen through the lens of social class – for instance, the mention of *operaiə* (factory workers), but also arguably low-middle class professions such as *docenti* (teachers), as well as female students (*studentesse*, seen as a homogeneous gendered group) – points at the schwa as an empty effort emerging from so-called *salotti femministi*. This expression frequently suggests that useless fights happen in higher social class circles, created by and for those who do not have to face class discrimination. I see this as one of the serendipity moments (as described by Partington et al., see Section 1.3.1), as it provides an opportunity to reflect on intersections and intersectionality. The tweet is written by a man whose bio suggests he is a professor at an Italian university, casting doubts that this is a personal experience (for gender and, arguably, class). It is more likely an attempt to dismiss the relevance of gender inclusive language, emphasising a class struggle to undermine feminist efforts and its relation to the working-class. While more research is needed on how allyship works, possibly rethinking the categories, I argue that this is an important lens through which speakers participate in the exchange of ideas and values on Twitter.

2.5.3 Exploring the Corpus Ethnographically: Functions of Gender Inclusive Language

In this subsection of the analysis, I report on uses of the schwa that refer to *social* functions, where social refers to both how society is perceived and valued in linguistic choices as well as the medium in which these functions occur (Twitter). I unravel how the schwa is deliberately employed to convey several aspects of interactional work on Twitter through a corpus-assisted exploration of concordance lines that appeared while conducting the aforementioned investigations. In other words, these are qualitative *notes* that I made along the way, similar to those of an ethnographer that explores what happens in a site. While cherry-picking elements cannot be excluded, as for the discussion in the previous analysis, these are to be considered as an illustration of plausible functions in this corpus. They must not be considered the only functions, as others might emerge in different corpora. The more obvious function that is found in the corpus is that of self-representation. That can be seen as a way for people to, perhaps indirectly, *tell* their gender story, as in ((19)–(21)):

(19) In questo scenario io sono **l'amicǝ.INCL** che parla della serie. GIF
   In this case, I am the friend who talks about the TV series. GIF

(20) Ti sbagli! Mi sono **trasferitǝ.INCL** in Lussemburgo dopo il master!
   You're mistaken. I moved to Luxembourg after the MA programme!

(21) E pensare che dopo questo mi sono **fidanzatǝ.INCL** e ho trovato lavoro senza volerlo GIF
   And right after this I found a partner and a job without looking for them. GIF

In (19) – (21), the individuals posting on Twitter use the schwa to talk about themselves, suggesting they do not wish to be identified with feminine or masculine morphemes. Using the schwa can be seen as different while sharing some elements of more traditional coming out stories. In (19), there are mismatches – for example, the article preceding *amicǝ*, which can be a reference to the binary, whether feminine (stemming from *l'amica*) or masculine (*l'amico*). Perhaps because of this versatility, it is seen as inclusive, not having a gendered morpheme visible. On other occasions, the schwa is used to construct specific communities to which individuals participate or belong, as in the case of LGBTQIA+ ones, of which (22) and (23) are examples:

(22) BUON PRIDE MONTH A **TUTTǝ.INCL**!
   Happy Pride Month to all!

(23) Siamo **amicǝ.INCL, colleghǝ.INCL, vicinǝ.INCL** di casa, genitori.**EPIC, figliǝ. INCL** che chiedono a gran voce di essere **riconosciutǝ.INCL** e **tutelatǝ.INCL** 👉 milanopride.it
   We are friends, colleagues, neighbours, parents, children who are asking, in a loud voice, to be recognised and legally protected 👉 milanopride.it

In these examples, the schwa takes an added meaning as it constructs a specific group of people. In (22) and (23), the groups mentioned through the schwa seem to represent various identities in the gender and sexuality spectrum, as seen with reference to the pride event in Milan. It is possibly unsurprising that the identification with these groups is made visible through the schwa.

On the subject of political allyship, the mainstream left-wing PD has never openly spoken about gender inclusive language, and its website carries traces of generic masculines – for example, *i deputati, i senatori, gli eurodeputati* (the MPs and MEPs). Conversely, a smaller political party, arguably not mainstream, Possibile, uses the schwa to signal its stance and as a direct allyship tool (see Section 2.5.2). In (24), I present an example:

(24) Bologna Possibile partecipa alla piazza #MOLTOPIUDIZAN prevista per questo sabato alle ore 12:00 insieme a **tuttə.INCL lə.INCL compagnə.INCL** del #RivoltaPride contro l'affossamento del #DDLZan al Senato.
Bologna Possibile takes part in the #moltopiudizan mobilisation, on Saturday at 12 together with all comrades of #RivoltaPride against the collapse of the #DDLZan in the Upper Chamber.

In this example, the main inclusive term is *compagnə* (comrades), reproducing a linguistic item associated with left-wing parties in the past. The novelty of the inclusive device further suggests where the party stands in relation to the LGBTQIA+ community. The choice of the schwa is here related to how the political party aims to connect with the Twitter audience. Similarly, Burnett and Pozniak (2021) found that the *écriture inclusif* is used as a political tool, where French universities with a left-wing activism seemed more inclined to use the *point médian* (while those aligning with the right used binary forms, e.g., parentheses). In Formato and Somma (2023), we also explore how inclusive language can be used in or be meaningful in sociolinguistic communities, specifically Communities of Practice, Speech Communities, and Imagined Communities. The renegotiation of gendered terms touches on several aspects of traditional uses of masculine generics. For instance, in Formato (2019: 69), I noticed that some terms used in their masculine forms indicated a role rather than a person. While still anchored to a history that saw men suitable for specific professions, personalised masculines would go further than addressing or describing a woman in a traditionally male job. In other words, these terms would become a representation of the job or the professional category (e.g., *per essere il sindaco*.masc/to be a mayor). Speakers, through the schwa, are also able to renegotiate this view, as in (25):

(25) Nel futuro non ci servono così tanti.**MASC ingegnerə.INCL. Educatorə.INCL, medicə.INCL, infermierə.INCL, psicologə.INCL**, caretakers in generale, **artistə. INCL** ecc.. sono queste le figure di cui avremo più bisogno
In the future, we won't need so many engineers. Educators, doctors, nurses, therapists, caretakers, broadly speaking, artists, etc … are the professions we would need the most.

Replacing these masculine forms with inclusive ones shows how speakers envision a society that is more inclusive and different from a known gendered order regarding the suitability of gendered workforces. However, *tanti* (many) is still used in its masculine form, demonstrating that mismatches still occur (see Section 2.5.1).

In terms of how the schwa collaborates with other linguistic devices, the corpus offers some examples, such as the use of mixed inclusive forms, as in (26):

(26) Ah quindi è stato assunto per fare il.**MASC** baby sitter **a*.INCL figliə.INCL** di **qualcun*.INCL.**

  Ok, this means he has been hired to babysit someone's child.

In (26), there are three inclusive elements: the *preposizione articolata* (*a**), the noun (*figliə*), and the indefinite pronoun (*qualcun**). It is difficult to interpret why the speaker has decided to alternate the inclusive forms; perhaps it was easier for the *preposizione articolata*, while *qualcun–* would have worked similarly with both the schwa and the asterisk. I perceive this as a sign of flexibility that could be useful for the speakers to have their message on where they stand to come across (as also seen in Slemp, 2020 and Burnett and Pozniak, 2021).

Overcoming the personalised masculine (as in (25)) and the mixed form (as in (26)) is part, in my view, of how the schwa could become, for some speakers, a new generic, de facto substituting the sexist masculine one, which is fairly seen as a loaded legacy of the past. This is not to say that other strategies do not have the same potential on their own or in coexistence with others, and other strategies might as well emerge in the future. Burnett and Pozniak (2021: 810), starting from their investigation of the *point médian* in French, similarly believe that gender inclusive language has the potential of 'eliminating, or at least reducing, linguistic androcentrism'.

A confident competence is also found when speakers are called to reproduce gender and specific referents, as in (27):

(27) Io, mio.**MASC** padre.**MASC**, i.**MASC** miei.**MASC** fratelli.**MASC**, le.**FEM** mie. **FEM** nonne.**FEM**, la.**FEM** mia.**FEM** amica.**FEM**, lə.**INCL** miə.**INCL** amicə. **INCL,** gente su Facebook a cui ho chiesto in un gruppo. GIF

  Myself, my father, my brothers, my grandmothers, my friend, my friends, people on Facebook whom I contacted through a group. GIF

In this example, it is clear that the speaker is *in control* of the representation of gender in linguistic terms, showing that gender inclusive language does not erase women. The range of participants referred to in this tweet shows a certain flexibility in using gender inclusive language and in signalling the gender of the specific people (*mio padre, i miei fratelli, le mie nonne*) and groups (*lə miə amicə*). Here, *gente* (people) follows the idea of language neutralisation in constructing groups where gender is not made visible (cfr, the debate on terminology in Sections 1 and 2.3).

Another aspect found while exploring the corpus is the replacement of idiomatic forms through the inclusive schwa. With idiomatic expressions, I intend those usually understood as conventional; the speakers recognise the expression as familiar and having a specific meaning. In this case, the idiom

I found is *chiedo per unə amicə* (asking for a friend); this is a very common expression used on social media to pretend that the question asked does not stem from or concern the person asking, who instead becomes an intermediate for someone else – that is, an unnamed friend. Having checked the corpus, the grammatical gender in the idiomatic expression sometimes matches that of the speaker – for example, *chiedo per un'amica* for a female speaker. At the same time, in other cases, the masculine or masculine generic form, *chiedo per un amico*, is used. The willingness to (re)create groupness and connectedness through a request for interaction is core in social media. From this perspective, Leppänen et al. (2014: 113) describe social media as an 'affinity space' where what occurs originates from 'shared interests, causes, lifestyles, activities and cultural products with short life spans or passing popularity'. The timeliness is central to the aforementioned expression (*chiedo per unə amicə*), which can be seen as a 'cultural product' that could work in face-to-face interactions too. The expression is, therefore, a search for alignment in the *togetherness* of communities on Twitter. Regarding alignment, Zappavigna (2014: 139) explains that microblogging (the practice of posting on social media) revolves around 'share quotidian experience by conferring upon the private realm of daily experience a public audience'. This fits with what *chiedo per unə amicə* does, with the quest to start a conversation. Similarly, I find the idea of phatic communion, reframed by Zappavigna (2014) in the social media context, interesting: communication is centred around establishing bonds rather than merely or exclusively communicating ideas. Furthermore, the notion of a phatic media culture is telling, where bonds and sociability are the main objectives in a wide network (worldwide) (Zappavigna, 2014). More significant, in the context of social media, posts by individuals are an 'I am here' declaration, what Makice (2009) defines as 'linguistic ping'. For this reason, I argue that using the inclusive form, *chiedo per unə amicə*, is an explicit way to frame the individual's choices behind the 'I am here', one that supports the vision behind the inclusive device.

In exploring the term *carə* through concordance lines and manual analysis, I noticed that it was employed to refer to different groups involved in less or more proximity to the speaker. This is not to say that the forms *cara*.fem.sing, *care*.fem.plur, *caro*.masc.sing, *cari*.masc.plur (dear) are not used symmetrically to *carə*. *Carə*, in this corpus, was found to address the internet community and specific people with whom the speakers wish to interact through the mention function (@userhandle). On some occasions, *carə* was used to mean someone's loved ones or in a personal form (*carə me/dear me*). However, in addressing the internet community, we have two additional functions, which are (a) addressing the whole community to build a similar bond to that in (27), shown in example

(28), or (b) addressing the whole community to advertise a product or an event, as in (29), sharing information on an event on data mining.

(28) **carə.INCL**, vorrei andare anche io al mare . . .
     dear, I would like to go to the seaside too . . .

(29) **Amicə.INCL carə.INCL**, a giorni torniamo da voi con l'indirizzo esatto, e anche qualche suggerimento sulle zone di Catania.
     Dear friends, we will soon inform you of the right address and some recommendations about Catania.

What emerges from these tweets is the interactional nature of the discussion on Twitter, the search to build communities with strangers and known people. This is a specific feature of the schwa on Twitter: the written register and the multiple options for the speakers to recreate the welcoming space embedded in the use of the schwa. Similarly to previous functions, I also captured the use of the schwa for humour:

(30) Cosa dice **unə.INCL contadinə.INCL a suə.INCL figliə.INCL** quando fa battute idiote sul campo? Piantala
     What does a farmer say to their children when they make stupid jokes in the fields? Plant it!

This joke does not work in English, as *piantala* in Italian means both 'plant it' and 'stop it'. I did not recognise this joke as conventional, nor did it appear on Google, which I consulted to check whether its standard version was in the masculine form, as other conventional jokes. This means that the power of the schwa is pervasive; it enters different domains of communicative events and functions.

To sum up, the functions of the schwa observed in the corpus are as follows: self-representation, representation of the self in a wider group, construction of specific and internet communities, flexibility in alternating gender inclusive devices as well as in making gender visible in relation to different referents, social media idioms and jokes. This proves that creativity is at the core of this linguistic experiment, despite the criticisms of the schwa being limited and limiting its potential in substituting traditionally gendered morphemes.

3 Triangulation and Reflexivity

In these concluding remarks, I provide a reading of what was discussed in Section 2 from the triangulation between CADS and FCDA, set at the beginning of this Element. In addition, I also use this space to reflect on my position before, during and after the investigation of the schwa.

3.1 CADS and FCDA: Triangulating the Findings

Throughout this Element, I have made the *gendered* social context central to the investigation of gender inclusive language because of its strong connection with societal changes from an individual and a collective point of view. Both CADS and FCDA demand that what is outside the corpus, specifically gendered imbalances, is the lens through which language is observed. Starting from this, what can language tell us about the social issue at hand – that is, constructions and representation of new identities under the umbrella terms 'gender' and 'sexuality'? Firstly, the corpus did not solely assist the investigation of gender inclusive language but, being a specialised one, had at its core micro and macro sociolinguistic elements. I suggest it was an FCDA-oriented corpus as much as a CADS one, stemming from the idea that gender was not *an accident* in examining language but the focal starting point. More so, gender is seen through the lens of personal and collective legitimation, what Lazar (2005, 2007, 2014, 2017) refers to as a feminist political imagination (the first principle of FCDA) and Baker (2018) calls issues of social justice. Social justice and feminist political imagination are visible in using the schwa for personal narratives and, more deeply, in renegotiating a sexist generic language that benefits communities and society outside the self. Through an arguably small linguistic unit, there is a deliberate construction of a new imagination. The use of the schwa as a generic has been seen as a weakness of the goal of gender inclusivity (e.g., in Thornton, 2022) as it would not only cover the needs of a specific community, encasing the debate in a negationist frame (as discussed by Russell, 2024). Similarly, the negationist frame explains why some linguists (e.g., Arcangeli) are concerned with the technicalities rather than the functions of gender inclusive language. Coupland and Jaworski (2012) convincingly argue that language cannot be assumed merely to be a set of structural forms isolated from human and social functioning. Furthermore, elements of nostalgia and progressphobia (as described in Section 1) can also be considered in how gender inclusive language is rejected.

Conversely, I argue that the vision of the schwa and, the fact that it *shakes* the power of the generic masculine order, shows the freedom and strength of the linguistic item concerning allyship, empathy, and communion, and this must be thought of in connection with the broader social project that involves language and other actions (as in the fourth principle of FCDA). This must also be connected to the ongoing battle, started in the 1970s for English and later for other languages (late 1980s for Italian, see Formato, 2019) to expose and destabilise androcentric and sexist language. In the words of CADS, the schwa performs its crucial social function. Languagers, or rather genderers (Russell and Kinsley, 2024), create a welcoming space in opposition to the cultural and institutional discrimination seen in a society that attempts to repatriarchalise (Bogetić, 2022b) itself by re-establishing profound historical gendered imbalances and asymmetries. More specifically, the complexity of this scenario lies in the tension between a sexist, homophobic cis-hetero state and *a* new order, as also shown in the discussion of material external to the corpus (as per CADS) yet relevant to understanding the specific social fabric (as in the second principle of FCDA, 2007, 2014). In this, the element of moral panic cannot be disregarded, as far-right groups and parties (in Italy and all over the world) are fiercely using gender-inclusive language to re-establish the status quo which is seen under threat as well as installing the fear of the difference and a malevolent unknown.

In the challenge of and resistance towards old and sexist habitual mechanisms (Sczesny et al., 2015), speakers find a voice that becomes meaningful at micro levels, constructing the self and others and macro levels. Resistance work (as for the third principle of FCDA) is seen in the creativity, versatility, and flexibility of using the schwa in the tweets (Section 2.5.1). While there is a legacy of a generic masculine routine (with, e.g., masculine forms preceding schwa-words), more generally, this can be considered in a pool of options used by the speakers that are navigating given recommendations (as those by Gheno and Boschetto) and their affordability. The traces *left* in the corpus (and the sub-corpora) show that speakers are using this space competently, as shown in three analyses that explore the use of this gender-inclusive strategy (Section 2.5.1), metalanguaging (Section 2.5.3), and the functions (Section 2.5.2). These three perspectives, intertwined, show how social work is done.

It is important to say that this investigation focuses on the use of language on a social media platform; therefore, claims about frequency and ways in which it is employed are limited to the medium and some of its characteristics, more prevalently, this being a space where people write. The written register is, to some extent, an *easier* space to experiment with language, especially when unfamiliar sounds are entering spoken repertoires with embedded attitudes and stereotypes. One cannot say that the schwa is taken on board by all speakers, as ways in which it is rejected are found in this specialised corpus (and outside of it).

Emerging from the medium is also the relevance of gender inclusive language on social media. Twitter is a community in which discourses outside this online community inhabit it. It is easy to see a deep connection between Twitter and the idea of an imagined community (a term coined by Anderson, 1983) where people seek alignment with others on specific ideas or beliefs and do not necessarily know each other. There is more to discuss (see Gruzd, Wellman, and Takhteyev, 2011). With different degrees of knowing and different degrees of aligning, social media allows people to signal ways in which speakers wish to participate in this micro-context and, more likely, outside of it. There is a move away from the *imagined* to become a practice-based community that helps people legitimise their way of seeing the world, for themselves and in relation to those who behave equally (however, we should not conclude that this is a Community of Practice, as intended by the seminal work started by Eckert and McConnell-Ginet, 1992). Speakers are not passive in this micro or sub-community (inside Twitter as a wider community built on some shared values); rather, they are contributors, and they feed this community. What I am suggesting here is not that the speakers who choose the schwa agree on all topics (such as politics) or are interested in the same lifestyle. Specifically, in using this linguistic and social item, they feed the social media community with certain cultural and social values attached to the schwa, including inclusivity. They are the constructors of what McMillan and Chavis (1986) refer to as a 'sense of community' in their review of the literature interested in communities in their traditional sense (a geographical space in which people interact). Their work (published before social media changed the landscape) is interesting because it provides nuances that help describe in detail what is the sense of community. Three are applicable in how the schwa contributes to maintaining the social (media) community, and these are: (a) *membership* – that is, speakers belong to the community, which is signalled by the participation and the tweets in the corpora; (b) *influence*, described as a sense of mattering (McMillan and Chavis, 1986: 9), this meaning that speakers make a difference in this community (through allyship, empathy, self-representation); and (c) *shared emotional connection* – that is, those who are using the schwa are possibly sharing similar personal experiences and are narrating this through the linguistic choice.

To conclude, the schwa is representative of the potential of gender inclusive language and must not be seen as the only option for people who move away from the binary and the binarism in language and society. Freedom of choosing ways in which representation of the self and others remains with the speakers. From this perspective, I wish to mention that, for instance, some communities might have preferred to keep the schwa to represent themselves rather than seeing it spread in the generic form.

3.2 Reflexivity and Positionality

Dean (2017: 8) suggests that if we do 'not recognise subjectivities or deny subjective influences or not think about the choices made in research and the reasons behind these choices [this] will inevitably lead to substantially less scientifically useful insights'. This quote is central to some reflections, offered here, on the interconnections between myself as a person and as a researcher. In growing into academia, I realised that there is an urgent need to understand where one stands concerning the topic explored, the data set chosen and collected, and the methods that followed. This concern is not exclusively mine: Consoli and Ganassin (2023) published an edited collection concerning reflexivity from various viewpoints. Starting from the accounts of the scholars included in the collection, I concur that reflexivity is linked to 'humanness', a well-thought notion that is seen, to some extent, in contrast with notions such as unbiased, objective, and rigorous. A similar concept is that of 'empathetic science' explained by Dean (2017: 1), perceived as moving away from 'social research [that] is too often the work of humans who have failed to account for their humanness while attempting to objectify other humans for study'. Specifically, humanness and empathy give us a chance 'to acknowledge the complexities that characterise our research journeys from start to finish' (Consoli and Ganassin, 2023: 2). *Embracing* reflexivity, life experiences and unique ways of understanding society are seen as embedded in research. Reflexivity, therefore, becomes a research tool (Sauntson, 2023) operationalised in studying social and linguistic phenomena.

Sauntson (2023: 172) conceptualises reflexivity as turning back, specifically as an 'ongoing self-awareness throughout the research process'. On 'turning back', Dean (2017) asks researchers to consider methodological, theoretical, disciplinary, practical, and personal choices. Reflexivity, then, takes the route of positionality, defined as 'the conditions of a socially given situation' (Dean, 2017: 8). Some of the positions that encouraged me to start this project have become stronger as time passed and, more episodes of gender-inclusive language were *happening* around me. This covers aspects of my personal views on the institutionalised discrimination suffered by LGBTQIA+ communities in Italy, a country which continuously chooses to reframe people within the female and male binary (in a dichotomous and essentialist way) and heterosexual relations (as discussed in Section 2.1), particularly in the current far-right government. This social awareness of what happens in Italy should also be seen through the lens of my migration history, as I have made the UK my second home; specifically, these years in the UK offered me the chance to see my country not only from the outside but also through a comparative lens. I recognise that similar attacks against the LGBTQIA+ communities occur in the UK, but important work is being done to build a welcoming society, which could become an example for Italy. Further, I believe that my identity as a cis heterosexual person positions myself as an ally rather than a community member. On this account, I recognise that I might have a limited view of the linguistic needs of LGBTQIA+ communities and that personal freedom about choosing a representative language for the self must remain in the speakers' power.

In relation to the geographical remarks about the schwa (see Sections 2.3 and 2.5.2), seen as *belonging* to southern regions of Italy, I could not disregard my experience as a speaker from the South; throughout my life, I have constantly felt that my accent and my dialect were subject to prejudice. For this reason, I firmly question whether the negative association with the geographical area was a purely *neutral* linguistic statement.

In addition, I have hopefully *practised* care and considered the humanness of the participants when handling the tweets of the corpora, recognising that some people might be vulnerable and subject to many forms of discrimination. I reflected on how to choose concordances in a way that would not put the posters at risk – for instance, excluding those tweets containing personal and sensitive stories. In doing so, I hope to have prioritised the speakers, especially those who resort to social media, to find a solidarity space. Another aspect is using English to explain how the Italian language operates and functions, choosing the terms and terminology to represent the language phenomenon under investigation, gender inclusive language, and translating the concordances. In Argyriou (2022), there are interesting insights into how trans, non-binary, and gender non-conforming subjectivities navigate languages other than English while also seeing English terms used in those languages. In the paper, the concept of *talking gender* is introduced, expanding on the well-known notion of *doing gender* (West and Zimmerman, 1987). I believe this could become central to investigating language in communities outside anglophone areas. In this Element, the issue is different. Yet the core argument can be adapted when translating the *speech* of someone I do not know and how I contribute to the literature and knowledge on the topic through English. As for the former, I concur with Argyrlou (2022: 401) in that translating embeds statements of gender, national, cultural, and linguistic identity. I, therefore, decided to introduce glosses in the Italian version for masculine, feminine, epicene and inclusive forms, foregrounding the language under investigation. On this topic, Argyrlou suggests: 'not that English is capable of erasing other languages, but rather that it is capable of managing them' (398). I hope I have made sure that readers attempt, as much as possible, to see the language investigated not as an appendix of English but as an entity on its own.

3.3 Further Research, Limitations, and Final Words

This study complements the others that are slowly emerging on the use of gender inclusive strategies and attitudes in Italian, and as shown, within the scholarship on other languages. However, further research is needed to examine how the schwa and other devices are used in contexts other than digital spaces – for instance, in schools, institutions, and teaching (in Italy and where Italian is taught). This is worthwhile, specifically in relation to the political (transnational) re-contextualisation of anti-gender ideas. In relation to the analysis presented here, no research is without limitations or compromises concerning methodological choices preceding and following the analysis. While I confidently argue that the corpus built has offered the opportunity to shed light on some important insights, I also recognise that it should be considered a partial view of how speakers use, understand, and conceptualise the schwa. Furthermore, only some schwa-words were selected, providing what might be speculations on the generalisability of flexibility and creativity. The constraints of this Element meant I could not always explore the corpus further or examine specific phenomena in full; however, more attempts were made but not reported in the final version.

References

Abbou, J. (2011). Double gender marking in French: A linguistic practice of antisexism. *Current Issues in Language Planning*, 12(1), 55–75.

Acanfora, F. (2020). La dversità è negli occhi di chi guarda. Superare il concetto di inclusione della diversità sul lavoro. www.fishcalabria.org/wp-content/uploads/2020/11/Fabrizio-Acanfora_La-diversit%C3%A0-%C3%A8-negli-occhi-di-chi-guarda_compressed.pdf.

Acarno, C. (2020). Corpus-assisted discourse studies. In A. De Fina & A. Georgakopoulou, eds., *The Cambridge Handbook of Discourse Studies*. Cambridge: Cambridge University Press, pp. 165–85.

Allen, S. H. & Mendez, S. N. (2018). Hegemonic heteronormativity: Toward a new era of queer family theory. *Journal of Family Theory & Review*, 10(1), 70–86.

Anderson, B. R. O. (1983). *Imagined Communities: Reflections on the Origin and Spread of Nationalism*. London: Verso.

Anderson, C. (2022). Pronouns and social justice in the linguistics classroom. *Journal of Language and Sexuality*, 11(2), 251–63.

Argyriou, K. (2022). Cross-cultural issues in trans terminology: Spanish and Greek applications of globalised language. *Gender and Language*, 16(4), 382–407.

Ashburn-Nardo, L. (2018). What can allies do? In A. Colella & E. King, eds., *The Handbook of Workplace Discrimination*. Oxford: Oxford University Press, pp. 373–86.

Baker, P. (2013). Will Ms ever be as frequent as Mr? A corpus-based comparison of gendered terms across four diachronic corpora of British English. *Gender and Language*, (4)1, 125–49.

Baker, P. (2018). Conclusion: Reflecting on reflective research. In C. Taylor & A. Marchi, eds., *Corpus Approaches to Discourse*. London: Routledge, pp. 281–92.

Baker, P., Hardie, A. & McEnery, A. (2006). *A Glossary of Corpus Linguistics*. Edinburgh: Edinburgh University Press.

Banegas, D. L. & López, M. F. (2021). Inclusive language in Spanish as interpellation to educational authorities. *Applied Linguistics*, 42(2), 342–46.

Bazeley, P. & Kemp, L. (2012). Mosaics, triangles, and DNA: Metaphors for integrated analysis in mixed methods research. *Journal of Mixed Methods Research*, 6, 55–72.

Bell, A. (2006). *The Guidebook to Sociolinguistics*. Oxford: John Wiley & Sons.

Benozzo, A. (2013). Coming out of the credenza: An Italian celebrity unveils his 'new' gay self. *Sexualities*, 16(3–4), 336–60.

Bogetić, K. (2022a). Politics of resignification: Central and Eastern European perspectives on language and gender. *Gender and Language*, 16(3), 195–215.

Bogetić, K. (2022b). Language, gender and political symbolics: Insights from citizen digital discourses on gender-sensitive language in Serbia. *Journal of Sociolinguistics*, 27(2), 1–21.

Bonnett, A. (2016). *The Geography of Nostalgia: Global and Local Perspectives on Modernity and Loss*. London: Routledge.

Bonnin, J. E. & Coronel, A. A. (2021). Attitudes toward gender-neutral Spanish: Acceptability and adoptability. *Frontiers in Sociology*, 6, 629616.

Booij, G. E. (2012). *The Grammar of Words: An Introduction to Linguistic Morphology*. 3rd edition. Oxford: Oxford University Press.

Borba, R. (2019). Gendered politics of enmity: Language ideologies and social polarisation in Brazil. *Gender and Language*, 13(4), 423–48.

Borba, R. (2022). Enregistering 'gender ideology': The emergence and circulation of a transnational anti-gender language. *Journal of Language and Sexuality*, 11(1), 57–79.

Borba, R., Hall, K. & Hiramoto, M. (2020). Feminist refusal meets enmity. *Gender and Language*, 14(1), 1–7.

Brezina, V., Weill–Tessier, P. & McEnery, A. (2020). *#LancsBox v. 5.x*. [software]. http://corpora.lancs.ac.uk/lancsbox.

Burnett, H. & Pozniak, C. (2021). Political dimensions of gender inclusive writing in Parisian universities. *Journal of Sociolinguistics*, 25(5), 808–31.

Calder, J. (2020). Language, gender and sexuality in 2019: Interrogating normativities in the field. *Gender & Language*, 14(4), 429–54.

Calder, J. (2022). Interrogating the role of the cisgender listening subject in the study of queer and trans voices. Lavender Language and Linguistics 28, University of Catania, 21–23 May.

Callahan, I. & Loscocco, K. (2023). The prevalence and persistence of homophobia in Italy. *Journal of Homosexuality*, 70(2), 228–49.

Cameron, D. (1995). *Verbal Hygiene*. Abingdon: Routledge.

Coady, A. (2022). Language ideologies in inclusive language debates in France (2000–22). *Attitudes towards Gender-Inclusive Language: A Multinational Perspective*. Queen Mary University of London, 8–9 September. http://qmul.pfalzgraf.net/coady-ppt.pdf.

Collins, P. H. (2019). *Intersectionality as Critical Social Theory*. Durham, NC: Duke University Press.

Conrod, K. (2020). Pronouns and gender in language. In K. Hall & E. Barrett, eds., *The Oxford Handbook of Language and Sexuality*. Oxford: Oxford University Press. https://doi.org/10.1093/oxfordhb/9780190212926.013.63.

Conrod, K. (2022). Variation in English gendered pronouns: Analysis and recommendations for ethics in linguistics. *Journal of Language and Sexuality*, 11(2), 141–64.

Consoli, S. & Ganassin, S. (eds.). (2023). *Reflexivity in Applied Linguistics: Opportunities, Challenges, and Suggestions*. Abingdon: Routledge.

Cordoba, S. (2022). *Non-binary Gender Identities: The Language of Becoming*. Abingdon: Routledge.

Coupland, N. & Jaworski (2012). Sociolinguistic perspectives on metalanguage: Reflexivity, evaluation and ideology. In A. Jaworski, N. Coupland & D. Galasinski, eds., *Metalanguage: Social and ideological perspectives*. Berlin: De Gruyter, pp. 1–51.

Crenshaw, K. W. (2017). *On intersectionality: Essential writings*. New York: New Press.

Crowley, A. (2022). Language ideologies and legitimacy among nonbinary YouTubers. *Journal of Language and Sexuality*, 11(2), 165–89.

Dame-Griff, E. C. (2022). What do we mean when we say 'Latinx?' Definitional power, the limits of inclusivity, and the (un/re) constitution of an identity category. *Journal of International and Intercultural Communication*, 15(2), 119–31.

Dean, J. (2017). *Doing Reflexivity: An Introduction*. Bristol: Policy Press.

Denzin, N. K. (1978). *The Research Act*. Chicago, IL: Aldine (Original work published 1970).

Di Cristofaro, M. (2023). *Corpus Approaches to Language in Social Media*. Abingdon: Routledge.

Eckert, P. & McConnell-Ginet, S. (1992). Think practically and look locally: Language and gender as community-based practice. *Annual Review of Anthropology*, 21(1), 461–88.

Egbert, J. & Baker, P. (2020). *Using Corpus Methods to Triangulate Linguistic Analysis*. Abingdon: Routledge.

Egbert, J. & Schnur, E. (2018). The role of the text in corpus and discourse analysis: Missing the trees for the forest. In C. Taylor & A. Marchi, eds., *Corpus Approaches to Discourse*. Abingdon: Routledge, pp. 159–73.

Evolvi, G. (2023). The World Congress of Families: Anti-gender Christianity and digital far-right populism. *International Journal of Communication*, 17, 2805–22.

Facchini, I. (2021). *Linguaggio non binario in interpretazione di conferenza: Uno studio sperimentale sull'applicabilità dello schwa in interpretazione consecutiva dall'inglese in italiano*. Unpublished MA Thesis. Università di Bologna.

Fielding, N. G. & Fielding, J. L. (1986). *Linking Data*. Beverly Hills, CA: Sage.

Flick, U. (2017). Mantras and myths: The disenchantment of mixed-methods research and revisiting triangulation as a perspective. *Qualitative Inquiry*, 23(1), 46–57.

Formato, F. (2014). *Language use and gender in the Italian parliament*. PhD thesis. Lancaster University. https://core.ac.uk/reader/42413990.

Formato, F. (2016). Linguistic markers of sexism in the Italian media: A case study of *ministra* and *ministro*. *Corpora*, 11(3), 371–99.

Formato, F. (2019). *Gender, Ideology and Discourse in Italian*. Basingstoke: Palgrave.

Formato, F. (forthcoming). How is gendered language commented on and explained? An overview of speakers supporting or rebelling against a gendered system-justification frame in Italian. In M. Venuti, F. Vigo & E. Campisi, eds., *Strategies of Inclusion and Exclusion in Online and Offline Interaction*. New York: Peter Lang.

Formato, F. & Somma, A. L. (2023). Gender inclusive language in Italy: A sociolinguistic overview. *Journal of Mediterranean and European Linguistic Anthropology*, 5(1), 22–40.

Formato, F. & Tantucci, V. (2020). Uno: A corpus linguistic investigation of intersubjectivity and gender. *Journal of Language and Discrimination*, 4(1), 51–73.

Gheno, V. (2022). *Femminili Singolari+ : Il Femminismo È nelle Parole*. Florence: Effequ.

Gillings, M., Mautner, G. & Baker, P. (2023). *Corpus-Assisted Discourse Studies*. Cambridge: Cambridge University Press.

González Vázquez, I., Klieber, A. & Rosola, M. (forthcoming). Beyond pronouns. Gender visibility and neutrality across languages. In A. Luvell and E. Lepore, eds., *Oxford Handbook of Applied Philosophy of Language*. Oxford: Oxford University Press.

Gruzd, A., Wellman, B. & Takhteyev, Y. (2011). Imagining Twitter as an imagined community. *American Behavioral Scientist*, 55(10), 1294–1318.

Hekanaho, L. (2022). A thematic analysis of attitudes towards English non-binary pronouns. *Journal of Language and Sexuality*, 11(2), 190–216.

Hine, C. (2000). *Virtual Ethnography*. London: Sage.

Hipkins, D. (2011). 'Whore-ocracy': Show girls, the beauty trade-off, and mainstream oppositional discourse in contemporary Italy. *Italian Studies*, 66(3), 413–30.

Jaworski, A., Coupland, N. & Galasinski, D. (eds.). (2012). *Metalanguage: Social and Ideological Perspectives*. Berlin: De Gruyter.

Kinsley, K. & Russell, E. (2024). *Redoing Linguistic Worlds: Unmaking Gender Binarities, Remaking Gender Pluralities*. Bristol: Multilingual Matters.

Kolek, V. (2022). Nonbinary Czech language: Characteristics and discourse. *Gender and Language*, 16(3), 265–85.

Konnelly, L., Bjorkman, B. M. & Airton, L. (2022). Towards an engaged linguistics: Nonbinary pronouns as a site of advocacy in research and teaching. *Journal of Language and Sexuality*, 11(2), 133–40.

Kosnick, K. (2019). The everyday poetics of gender-inclusive French: Strategies for navigating the linguistic landscape. *Modern & Contemporary France*, 27(2), 147–61.

Lange, M. B. (2022) Attitudes towards gender-fair language within German academia. Comparing positions adopted by university guidelines for gender-fair language with attitudes found amongst medical and gender researchers. *Attitudes towards Gender-Inclusive Language: A Multinational Perspective*. Queen Mary University of London, 8–9 September. http://qmul.pfalzgraf.net/lange-ppt.pdf.

Lazar, M. M. (2005). Politicizing gender in discourse: Feminist critical discourse analysis as political perspective and praxis. In M. M. Lazar, ed., *Feminist Critical Discourse Analysis*. Basingstoke: Palgrave, pp. 1–28.

Lazar, M. M. (2007). Feminist critical discourse analysis: Articulating a feminist discourse praxis. *Critical Discourse Studies*, 4(2), 141–64.

Lazar, M. M. (2014). Feminist critical discourse analysis. In S. Ehrlich, M. Meyerhoff & J. Holmes, eds., *The Handbook of Language, Gender and Sexuality*. Hoboken, NJ: Wiley Blackwell, pp. 180–99.

Lazar, M. M. (2017). Feminist critical discourse analysis. In J. Flowerdew & J. E. Richardson, eds., *The Routledge Handbook of Critical Discourse Studies*. Abingdon: Routledge, pp. 372–87.

Leap, W. L. (2003). Language and gendered modernity. In J. Holmes & M. Meyerhoff, eds., *The Handbook of Language and Gender*. Oxford: Blackwell, pp. 401–22.

Leppänen, S., Kytölä, S., Jousmäki, H., Peuronen, S. & Westinen, E. (2014). Entextualization and resemiotization as resources for identification in social media. In P. Seargeant & C. Tagg, eds., *The Language of Social Media: Identity and Community on the Internet*. Basingstoke: Palgrave Macmillan, pp. 112–36.

Lomotey, B. A. (2018). Making Spanish gender fair: A review of anti-sexist language reform attempts from a language planning perspective. *Current Issues in Language Planning*, 19(4), 383–400.

Maestri, G. & Somma, A.L. (2020). *Il Sessismo nella Lingua Italiana: Trent'anni Dopo Alma Sabatini*. Pavia: Blonk.

Makice, K. (2009). *Twitter API. Up and Running: Learn How to Build Applications with the Twitter API*. Sebastopol, CA: O'Reilly Media.

Marchi (2022). GET BACK! Retrieving nostalgia: Challenges of using CADS to analyse phenomena which defy lexicalisation. Corpora & Discourse International Conference. University of Bologna, 26–28 August.

McMillan, D. W. & Chavis, D. M. (1986). Sense of community: A definition and theory. *Journal of Community Psychology*, 14(1), 6–23.

Melendez, S. & Crowley, A. (2022). Pronoun practices in the higher education classroom. *Journal of Language and Sexuality*, 11(2), 264–77.

Mills, S. (2008). *Language and Sexism*. Cambridge: Cambridge University Press.

Mioni, A. M. & Arnuzzo-Lanszweert, A. M. (1979). Sociolinguistics in Italy. *International Journal of the Sociology of Language*, 21, 81–107.

Motschenbacher, H. (2014). Grammatical gender as a challenge for language policy: The (im)possibility of non-heteronormative language use in German versus English. *Language Policy*, 13, 243–61.

Nardone, C. (2018). 'Women and work': A cross-linguistic corpus-assisted discourse study in German and in Italian. *Critical Approaches to Discourse Analysis across Disciplines*, 10(1), 167–16.

Nartey, M. (2024). Women's voice, agency and resistance in Nigerian blogs: A feminist critical discourse analysis. *Journal of Gender Studies*, 33(4), 418–30.

Nodari, R. (2022) Attitudes and stereotypes of gender inclusive strategies in Italian. *Attitudes towards Gender-Inclusive Language: A Multinational Perspective*. Queen Mary University of London, 8–9 September. http://qmul.pfalzgraf.net/nodari-ppt.pdf.

Partington, A. (2003). Book review: Gillings, M. et al. (2023) *Corpus-Assisted Discourse Studies. Cambridge Element. Journal of Corpora and Discourse Studies*, 6(1), 53–60.

Partington, A. (2006). Metaphors, motifs and similes across discourse types: Corpus-Assisted Discourse Studies (CADS) at work. In A. Stefanowitsch & S. T. Gries, eds., *Corpus-based Approaches to Metaphor and Metonymy*. Berlin: Mouton de Gruyter, pp. 267–304.

Partington, A. (2023). Book review: Gillings, M., Mautner, G. & Baker, P. (2023) *Corpus-Assisted Discourse Studies*. Cambridge Elements. *Journal of Corpora and Discourse Studies*, 6(1), 53–60.

Partington, A., Duguid, A. & Taylor, C. (2013). *Patterns and Meanings in Discourse: Theory and Practice in Corpus-Assisted Discourse Studies (CADS)*, vol. 55. Amsterdam: John Benjamins.

Paterson, L. (2019). Interview with Erin Carrie and Rob Drummond of the Accentism Project. *Journal of Language and Discrimination*, 3(1), 76–84.

Paterson, L. (ed.). (2023). *The Routledge Handbook of Pronouns*. Abingdon: Routledge.

Pauwels, A., & Winter, J. (2006). Gender inclusivity or 'grammar rules OK'? Linguistic prescriptivism vs linguistic discrimination in the classroom. *Language and Education*, 20(2), 128–40.

Pershai, A. (2017). The language puzzle: Is inclusive language a solution? In A. Braithwaite & C. Orr, eds., *Everyday Women's and Gender Studies*. Abingdon: Routledge, pp. 55–8.

Pierucci, M.C. (2021) Car* tutt*: Degli usi dell'asterisco di genere nelle scritture pubbliche, fra diniego consapevole e adozione spontanea. In R. Bombi, ed., *La Comunicazione Istituzionale ai Tempi della Pandemia: Da Sfida a Opportunità*. Rome: Il Calamo, pp. 193–206.

Popič, D. & Gorjanc, V. (2018). Challenges of adopting gender-inclusive language in Slovene. *Suvremena Lingvistika*, 44(86), 329–50.

Postill, J. & Pink, S. (2012). Social media ethnography: The digital researcher in a messy web. *Media International Australia*, 145(1), 123–34.

Raby, R. (2005). What is resistance? *Journal of Youth Studies*, 8(2), 151–71.

Radke, H. R., Kutlaca, M., Siem, B., Wright, S. C. & Becker, J. C. (2020). Beyond allyship: Motivations for advantaged group members to engage in action for disadvantaged groups. *Personality and Social Psychology Review*, 24(4), 291–315.

Renström, E. A., Lindqvist, A. & Sendén, M.G. (2022). The multiple meanings of the gender-inclusive pronoun hen: Predicting attitudes and use. *European Journal of Social Psychology*, 52(1), 71–90.

Rosola, M. (in preparation). Gender-fair strategies in Italian between visibility and neutrality.

Russell, E. (2024). Ciro è morto o morta? Symbolic power and discursive effablity. In K. Kinsley & E. Russell, eds., *Redoing Linguistic Worlds: Unmaking Gender Binarities, Remaking Gender Pluralities*. Bristol: Multilingual Matters, pp. 269–301.

Safina E. S. (forthcoming). 'I NOSTRX CORPX RESISTONO': A corpus analysis of Italian gender neutralization strategies in transfeminist online communities. In S. Burnett & F. Vigo, eds., *Battlefield Linguistics: Contemporary Contestations of Language, Gender, and Sexuality*. Berlin: De Gruyter-Mouton.

Sauntson, H. (2023). Reflexivity, emerging expertise, and Mi[S-STEP]s: A collaborative self-study of two TESOL teacher educators. In S. Consoli & S. Ganassin, eds., *Reflexivity in Applied Linguistics: Opportunities, Challenges and Suggestions*. Abingdon: Routledge, pp. 171–89.

Scharrón-del Río, M. R. & Aja, A. A. (2020). Latinx: Inclusive language as liberation praxis. *Journal of Latinx Psychology*, 8(1), 7–20.

Sczesny, S., Moser, F. & Wood, W. (2015). Beyond sexist beliefs: How do people decide to use gender-inclusive language? *Personality and Social Psychology Bulletin*, 41(7), 943–54.

Shaw, S. (2020). *Women, Language and Politics*. Cambridge: Cambridge University Press.

Sheydaei, I. (2021). Gender identity and nonbinary pronoun use: Exploring reference strategies for referents of unknown gender. *Gender and Language*, 15(3), 369–93.

Slemp, K. (2021). Attitudes towards varied inclusive language use in Spanish on Twitter. *Working Papers in Applied Linguistics and Linguistics at York*, 1, 60–74. https://wally.journals.yorku.ca/index.php/default/article/view/6.

Slemp, K., Black, M. & Cortiana, G. (2020). Reactions to gender-inclusive language in Spanish on Twitter and YouTube. *Actes du congrès annuel de l'Association canadienne de linguistique 2020. Proceedings of the 2020 Annual Conference of the Canadian Linguistic Association*. https://cla-acl .ca/pdfs/actes-2020/Slemp_Black_Cortiana_CLA-ACL2020.pdf.

Somma, A. L. (2023). Whatsapp audio to Federica Formato, 14 April.

Sulis, G. & Gheno, V. (2022). The debate on language and gender in Italy, from the visibility of women to inclusive language (1980s–2020s). *The Italianist*, 42(1), 153–83.

Taylor, C. & Marchi, A. (2018). *Corpus Approaches to Discourse: A Critical Review*. Abingdon: Routledge.

Thornton, A. (2022). Genere e igiene verbale: L'uso di forme con ǝ in italiano. *Annali del Dipartimento di Studi Letterari, Linguistici e Comparati. Sezione linguistica*, 11, 11–54.

Tusting, K. (ed.). (2019). *The Routledge Handbook of Linguistic Ethnography*. Abingdon: Routledge.

Varis, P. & Hou, M. (2019). Digital approaches in linguistic ethnography. In K. Tusting, ed., *The Routledge Handbook of Linguistic Ethnography*. Abingdon: Routledge, pp. 229–40.

Vergoossen, H. P., Pärnamets, P., Renström E. A. & Gustafsson Sendén, M. (2020). Are new gender-neutral pronouns difficult to process in reading? The case of hen in Swedish. *Frontiers in Psychology*, (11), 574356.

West, C. & Zimmerman, D. H. (1987). Doing gender. *Gender and Society*, 1(2), 125–51.

Zappavigna, M. (2014). Coffee tweets: Bonding around the bean on Twitter. In P. Seargeant & C. Tagg, eds., *The Language of Social Media: Identity and Community on the Internet*. Basingstoke: Palgrave Macmillan, pp. 139–10.

Zappavigna, M. (2017). Twitter. In C. R. Hoffmann & W. Bublitz, eds., *Pragmatics of Social Media*. Berlin: De Gruyter, pp. 201–24.

Zimman, L. (2017). Transgender language reform: Some challenges and strategies for promoting trans-affirming, gender-inclusive language. *Journal of Language and Discrimination*, 1(1), 84–105.

To Aisha and Francesco

Cambridge Elements ☰

Language, Gender and Sexuality

Helen Sauntson
York St John University

Helen Sauntson is Professor of English Language and Linguistics at York St John University, UK. Her research areas are language in education and language, gender and sexuality. She is co-editor of *The Palgrave Studies in Language, Gender and Sexuality* book series, and she sits on the editorial boards of the journals *Gender and Language* and the *Journal of Language and Sexuality*. Within her institution, Helen is Director of the Centre for Language and Social Justice Research.

Holly R. Cashman
University of New Hampshire

Holly R. Cashman is Professor of Spanish at University of New Hampshire (USA), core faculty in Women's and Gender Studies, and coordinator of Queer Studies. She is past president of the International Gender and Language Association (IGALA) and of the executive board of the Association of Language Departments (ALD) of the Modern Languages Association. Her research interests include queer(ing) multilingualism and language, gender, and sexuality.

About the Series

Cambridge Elements in Language, Gender and Sexuality highlights the role of language in understanding issues, identities and relationships in relation to multiple genders and sexualities. The series provides a comprehensive home for key topics in the field which readers can consult for up-to-date coverage and the latest developments.

Cambridge Elements ≡

Language, Gender and Sexuality

Elements in the Series

The Language of Gender-Based Separatism: A Comparative Analysis
Veronika Koller, Alexandra Krendel and Jessica Aiston

Queering Sexual Health Translation Pedagogy
Piero Toto

Legal Categorization of 'Transgender': An Analysis of Statutory Interpretation of 'Sex', 'Man', and 'Woman' in Transgender Jurisprudence
Kimberly Tao

LGBTQ+ and Feminist Digital Activism: A Linguistic Perspective
Angela Zottola

Feminism, Corpus-Assisted Research, and Language Inclusivity
Federica Formato

A full series listing is available at: www.cambridge.org/ELGS

Printed in the United States
by Baker & Taylor Publisher Services